PRESS INTO THE POWER

A Journey to Healing and Breakthrough

DEREK L. CALHOUN

This book is a work of non-fiction. Unless otherwise noted, the author and the publisher make no explicit guarantees as to the accuracy of the information contained in this book and in some cases, names of people and places have been altered to protect their privacy.

WestBow Press books may be ordered through booksellers or by contacting:

WestBow Press
A Division of Thomas Nelson & Zondervan
1663 Liberty Drive
Bloomington, IN 47403
www.westbowpress.com
844-714-3454

ISBN: 978-1-6642-5794-8 (sc)
ISBN: 978-1-6642-5795-5 (hc)
ISBN: 978-1-6642-5796-2 (e)

Library of Congress Control Number: 2022902889

Print information available on the last page.

WestBow Press rev. date: 06/17/2022

CONTENTS

PANDEMIC LITERATURE

In every period of life, dating back to the early stages and formation of written communication, literature has been written that is common to its era. This literature explains these times in human history consistent with its tragedies and triumphs. From ancient history to this postmodern era we currently live in, literature has been birthed and produced congruent with the major events of each epoch of time. This time period is no different from any other. The literature of this time is reflective of a world pandemic, financial crisis, and a fleeting way of life that is yielding to this cataclysmic social economic revolution. As my wife often reminds me, a new normal is emerging. Thus, I write as a participant observer from the vantage point of watching everything change around us, but there is one constant throughout the ages, and that is the sovereignty of our God. Hence, the Hebrew writer penned these words in the canon:

Jesus Christ is the same yesterday, today, and forever.
—Hebrews 13:8 (NKJV)

GRACE AND GRATITUDE

Nothing happens in this world without the consent of Almighty God. It is His grace that overshadows me and allows me the insight, power, and presence of Spirit to write as I have written now and over the course of my life. We can take credit for nothing, because all good and perfect gifts come down from the Father of the heavenly lights (James 1:17). I am grateful for the power of the Holy Spirit that navigate my fingers around the keys of this keyboard. Jesus Christ is the catalyst for anything good in my life. If this book blesses you, we owe it all to the magnified love of God that hedges or encloses us all (Psalm 139:5).

There is never a day that goes by that I do not recognize that I am who I am because of the marvelous grace of God. My life as I know it would have been impossible without the plan that God had for my life. I am blessed to be the son of James and the late Catherine H. Calhoun, who gave me love, nurturing support, and a moral foundation in life that cannot be shaken. I was raised with my baby sister, Mrs. Juandalynn A. Heslop, who from her teenage years to now is my greatest cheerleader and supporter. My parents surrounded us with both family and extended family, and they became our village in Hartford, Connecticut. They sacrificed to send us to the best schools their money could buy at that time. My parents also taught us the importance of learning how to speak the King's English and how to read and write correctly.

This foundation followed me through Northwest Catholic HS in W. Hartford, Connecticut. Later, I gained admittance to Cornell University, but I decided to embrace the hallowed halls of academia at the Howard University in Washington, DC. It was here that I majored in English and honed the gift of writing. However, my greatest accomplishment at Howard was developing a relationship with the Lord Jesus Christ. This decision altered the course of my life forever, and I have never been the same since then. This change fueled another major decision, and that was to choose the Howard University School of Divinity for graduate studies over the University of Baltimore School of Law.

While I was in DC, I found and married the queen of my dreams and the love of my life, Sharron L. Calhoun, and to us were born four lovely daughters, Brittanye, Candace, Taylor, and Vashti, whom I love dearly. I am grateful for each of their contributions to my life and my book. My wife has been the Rock of Gibraltar through every point in our lives, both good and bad, since I was nineteen years old. She was my First Lady before I pastored the Grace Baptist Church in Norwalk, Connecticut, or cofounded New Vision

International Ministries in Bridgeport, Connecticut, with my spiritual parents, Bishop Vaughn M. and Lady Narlene J. McLaughlin. Their sagacious mentorship, spiritual guidance, and keen insight and the altruistic support of the Potter's House International Ministries during that season of my life until today is nothing short of an outpouring of the perpetual love of God.

However, none of that would have been possible without God in my heart, my wife at my side, and a very gracious and supportive family. They all made tremendous amounts of sacrifice, and I owe them a debt of gratitude. Family means the world to me. I am graced to be a part of the Heard, Acres, Brooks, Mack, Calhoun, Jones, Heslop, and Briscoe families, anchored by the next generation, Josiah, Meila, and Jolie, my fabulous grandchildren.

During this journey, I have been blessed to meet a massive cadre of people from classmates to coworkers. Many have scaffolded me at various times in my life. If I tried to mention the names of all of these people, I would need to write another book, and I would inevitably miss some names, and that is the last thing I want to do. However, I do want to thank God for the grace of being able to work with, rub shoulders with, and sit at the feet of some of the most supportive, loving, kind, and brilliant people in the world. I thank God for you all!

I am blessed to be supported in prayer by a world-class intercessory team. I am encouraged by another circle of friends, who became the mouthpiece of God at just the right time. My prophetic inner circle is special; you have leaned on the breast of God and relayed divine insight that has helped to shape my life. Thanks to my technical team, who kept me on the cutting edge of technology down through the years. To my care team that met the needs of my family and parents in every way conceivable; we are blessed. I want to say that I am eternally grateful to every professional teacher, pastor, professor, mentor, boss, relative, and friend who took the time to teach me the lessons of life and classroom. Lastly, a very special thanks to my administrative team, led by the "Killer Bees," who have supported me for the last twenty-five years, typing, editing, scheduling travel arrangements, and generally keeping me on task, to say the least.

Special thanks to the Kingdom Influencing Network and all of my spiritual sons and daughters who are sprinkled around the United States. Especially to the faithful soldiers of New Vision International Ministries, under the direction of Pastors Dexter B. and Lady Lindsey J. Upshaw. There is no other church that has added as much to the context of my life and the life of my family. Thank-you for being uber supportive to this very day! Please continue to lead and be a beacon of light in the Northeast. Kudos to the team at WestBow Press and my new marketing and public relations consortium. Thank you and blessings in advance to everyone who will support this project. I could not do this without your patronage and support.

In closing, here is what I want to say to all of you mentioned or unmentioned but never forgotten in the heart of God. I realize that I am a compendium of all the people who have ever added value to my life. Value can be added by both negative and positive influences, based on the calculations of the omniscient God we serve. So with humility of heart and the grace and gratitude afforded me through my Lord and Savior, Jesus Christ, I want to close by saying thank you to all from the very depths of my soul! May this book bless the lives of every reader and listener until God returns to get us all!

PS If it really touched or blessed your life, tell at least three people about the book, or purchase one for them! Thanks again!

MEMORIAM

Bishop Lewis T. Tait Sr.
Pastor George Exum
Pastor Joseph A. Gilmore Sr.
Elder Malcolm Skeeter
Elder Glenn Williams
Deacon John Harris Sr.
Dr. Cain Hope Felder
Dr. Charles Green
Dean Dr. Lawrence M. Jones
Henderson & Alora Acres
Mattie Armstead
Joseph & Naomi Brooks
George & Luanne Blagrove
Catherine H. Calhoun
Hattie Calhoun
Mary Grissette
Sarah Hardy
Jack & Emma Heard
Lillie Hendricks
Lazarus & Inez Jones
Moses & Anne Mack
Elbert & Christine Williams

I realize that a man is the sum total of all of his experiences in life, both good and bad. Thus, to acknowledge some of the people in my life who have gone on to be with the Lord and yet played critical roles in the formation of my character and this book is a foregone conclusion.

I especially want to dedicate this book to my dad, James Calhoun Jr., and my mom, the late Catherine Calhoun. They were an indomitable force in my growth and development, and they never wavered in making sure they did their part as educators (private tutors) and parents who set parameters for morality and lines of demarcation for living in their home.

They taught me the power of responsibility by waking me up at six o'clock on Saturday mornings to do chores at the age of ten. They were responsible for developing a work ethic in me by making sure I had my first real job experience at twelve, working with Mr. Williams landscaping in order to earn my keep. This was a critical time in my adolescent formation, especially in the area of executive decision-making. Finally, my parents created an organic culture of reading, writing, and arithmetic—or what they referred to as the three Rs. This was part of a discipline that was instilled in me during my elementary years. Thank you, Mom and Dad, for your love and support!

FOREWORD

Grace and peace to you from God our Father. I have not had the privilege of meeting you, but together we are bonded together by the saving blood of Jesus Christ. It is in His name I greet you and am excited to share my full conviction that in the next few pages, you will begin to unwrap a gift from God that He has imparted through the wisdom of Bishop Derek L. Calhoun. Without a doubt, I know in my heart that beyond this foreword, you will embark on a transformative journey. A journey that will undoubtedly be the catalyst for how God desires to both stretch and shape you deeper into His will! You have no idea how pastorally proud and excited I am for your journey. I know that as soon as you open yourself to what God desires to say to you, you will be released into a dynamically rich and rewarding relationship, uncovering new dimensions of your created self in the image of our God. In prayer and with patience, pace yourself to read what will cause you to pause so that God can meet you in your garden and prune your life in such a way that an increase of abundant fruit may come forth. If there is one place I know for sure where you can be transparently honest about your journey, it is in this great work written by Bishop Derek L. Calhoun, titled *Press into the Power.*

How am I assured? Because I know Bishop, but greater still, I know the voice of God and how He has used the wisdom imparted to Bishop to completely transmogrify my very life! Though you may be meeting Bishop Calhoun for the first time through the words on these pages, I encourage you to receive him. Allow him to be the messenger on assignment by God to agitate you out of stagnation and comfort. His intent is to aid you in learning how to press into the power!

Now the question you are most likely asking is what makes this book any different than the thousands of books written on the subject. The answer is easy. It is the quality and the character of the author, who prophetically has received a right-now Word from God that will resonate in your heart and is relevant for the times we are currently navigating. The scripture tells us in summation in 1 John 4:1 that we are well encouraged to trust not in every spirit but to try the spirit by the spirit. If you are centered in God, you will be able to receive the impartation from God through one who many lovingly and reverentially refer to simply as "Bishop." The wisdom and anointing of God saturates the pages of this ministry offering and will flow into your life as the dew of Hermon.

Beloved, my mentor once told me that in life there are three people you need: a coach, a challenger, a confidant.

Bishop has a love for the Lord and God's people as I've never experienced. In my life, he has been a father, a coach, a mentor, a challenger, a confidant, and a critical eye, all of which is shaped through the hermeneutic of God's love. In short summation, Bishop is a gift, or as he would rather say, he wants to share with you a gift to grow you closer to *the gift*, which is a dynamic relationship with Christ.

As you unwrap the gift, it will yield a blessing in your life, making you fully available to God for God's greater purpose in your life's work. But understand this: the fulfilment of this journey doesn't come without a press, and the press can't make the transformational shift without power, so, my brothers and sisters, press into the power. Allow God greater access to fortify you as He dismantles the obstacles to perform a spiritual reset. This centrifugal connection is designed to pull your life *forward*!

I have great hope in this work because I know it has the power to make your life better, as it has mine, but reading alone won't make it so. You have got to learn a new skill, develop a new muscle, be both passionate and persistent, and you simply can't give up on God. Transparently, I first met Bishop and began receiving this instruction at an intersection in my life that I simply did not know how to navigate. I wanted to run backward. I wanted to run forward. I could not understand how God could love me and deliver me from what seemed to be a stagnant, no-win situation. Bishop helped me to see that running was not the answer; pressing was. The pages forthwith became an honest journey and joy for me to read. It allowed me the privacy to approach God and humbly stand before Him differently than Adam and Eve, apologetically and gratefully unashamed. It allowed me to hear from God and to know that through His love I am accepted, yet He still loves me to the point to develop so much more.

On the face of each page, in the leaves of this great work, you will hear the voice of one you may not know, called Bishop, but more importantly, within the fiber of every page, may you feel the whisper of God. It's not only possible. It's the incarnate prayer that I know Bishop has prayed in his journey to be a faithful witness. My purpose in writing this foreword is to let you know you can have assurance in what you read, because it conveys the truth of what God says. Not for self-aggrandizement, neither for fame nor notoriety, but in the truth of God's love, because Bishop would not write for any other reason than that. Often Bishop has told me to "wait for the sound." There is a sound that comes from heaven that will enable you to move even when you cannot see. Right now, you may hold this work in your hands at a moment in your life when giving up is easy; where frustration and fatigue have become parasitic to your soul; where you just aren't sure what to believe or, better still, are asking the question, "God, what are You saying?" Let Bishop be your spiritual coach, but most importantly, let the Lord guide your understanding. I promise you there was no nothing more compelling that has ushered him in this pursuit.

The maxim says, "no prayer, no power, know prayer, know power." Here's my advice: take the journey, get in your prayer position, and tunnel through whatever is in your path relentlessly. The only way to do so is to learn to first *press into the power.*

Let me get out of your way. There's so much before you to read that indeed is going to be a blessing. Take it not on my word—this word coming from heaven is sent to you by God. Both this message and this messenger will be a blessing as you take the next move. Faithfully unwrap the blessings of God and get started today. Press into the power!

—Dr. Dustin Berlack Sullivan, Founding Pastor, The New Life Church – Loudoun, Loudon County, Virginia

SECTION I

THE FOUNDATION

THE ACKNOWLEDGMENT

As I write this work, it is imperative that you, the reader, understand that I am not writing this book for fame or fortune. I am writing this as an oracle of God. I just want to write what I believe He is saying through me at this time. The salvation of souls is of course the main priority of the Father. However, there are many believers who have been saved for a long time, but they have slipped from their places of authority and power in God. Moreover, there are still those who wait impatiently under the wings of God. They are waiting for their moment of divine release.

Time has beaten them down. Religion and religious practices have consumed them with compromise. Their minds are filled with doubt, and their hearts ooze insecurity and fear. I know there are those in the body who will say, "This is not me!" Moreover, at the first sound of a seemingly defeatist posture, they put their guards up—but read on! There is something for all of us in this book, if we will be true to ourselves. How many times have you heard this statement when having a conversation with the saints: "When I first got saved, I was on fire!" Others say, "I am mature now, so it doesn't take all that!" Does maturity mean that we no longer hunger and thirst after righteousness? I am talking to the people who can look in the mirror and make an honest assessment, saying to themselves, "What happened to me?"

Life happened! Attacks of the enemy, wars in our members, a legion of lies, unfulfilled promises, brokenness, unchecked pain, the burden of debt, loss of loved ones, negative atmospheres, battles with the thorn in our flesh, sexual abuses, toxic relationships, unforgiveness, and an endless string of disappointments, just to name a few. Most of all, in the midst of it all, we lost connection with God. When we first found the Lord or received Christ in our life, we stayed in the face of God. We prayed and fasted with unbridled recklessness, contending for the faith, only wanting to please God. We believed God regardless of what we may have seen. We served God in season and out. Now we pray about everything and do nothing. We take prayer requests in good faith, and like a congressional bill, the requests die on Capitol Hill.

Lord, we acknowledge that we have not been the army that you have called us to be. We have taken off our armor, and we no longer want to go to battle. Generals of your army cry with tears of loneliness because the troops no longer want to fight. We are like Israel, during the days when King Saul sat under the pomegranate tree, waiting with a terrified army. They had no weapons and suffered from the spirit of dispersion and fear. However, a company of two started a revolution by pressing into the presence and power of God. Their faith and obedience put a demand on the power of God. We need to learn how to ask God to do something impossible. Sometimes God does not respond to our prayers because our vision is way too small.

Thus, these two men turned the tide of this conflict with the Philistines just by trusting God and taking a risk to be different from the rest of the army. Their obedience demonstrated the power and sovereignty of God even in the midst of imminent defeat in the natural realm. However, victory is always in the hands of those who put their trust in God! We must believe that the power of God is still as influential now as it was in the days of Jonathan! He and his armorbearer demonstrated an incredible amount of courage. They single-handedly defeated twenty Philistines in the span of a half acre of land (1 Samuel 14:1–14).

Looking at our current spiritual landscape, God sees a sea of "abandoned thrones" across the earth in this season. Abandoned thrones vacated by Christians who have abdicated their responsibilities in the marketplace and at home. Our witness has been corrupted and compromised by a virus of the politically correct who want to offend no one. Apologetics or contending for the faith is no longer a priority. We are infected by moral relativism, the deconstruction of the belief in any form of absolute truth. In other words, there is no right or wrong: it is all relative. Then came the COVID-19 pandemic, George Floyd protests around the world, and the day of infamy and insurrection at the US Capitol on January 6, 2021. Many were lost and lost hope, like the Israelites in the days of Jonathan. The pandemic and other ensuing life-altering events were not a call to run and hide. They were a call to regroup and rise out of the ashes of obscurity.

I am by no means suggesting that we are supposed to ignore the authorities, but we are supposed to heed the call of God to get closer to Him. We need specific instructions. We need new strategies. We need a Word from the Lord. We need wisdom to understand the times we are currently facing. We need to prepare for the next major disruption in the fabric of our lives. God is interrupting our regularly scheduled programing to get our attention because, like sheep, we have lost our way.

The pandemic, like postmodernism, has shaken the foundations of normalcy and religion. There has been a shift, and there will be a shift. God is calling us back to a place of repentance. The outer court will be full before these days are over. We will grow in the spirit of repentance. We will acknowledge the sins that have been integrated into our daily lifestyles.

Yes, God knows our hearts, and they are "evil continually" (Genesis 6:5 NKJV). This is not an indictment but an acknowledgment of why we all need forgiveness of our sins. We all need the Advocate to go before us. We all need the Savior, the Son of God, Jesus Christ. He did not give His life in vain. The resurrection was not in vain! We "all have sinned and fall short of the glory of God" (Romans 3:23 NKJV). It is true and written, "There is none righteous, no, not one!" (Romans 3:10 NKJV). Again, this is not a license to sin but a reflection of our need for forgiveness.

We acknowledge Your Word, Lord, and we acknowledge our need to turn away from sin, mediocrity, and compromise and to turn back to the excellency of Your presence and resurrection power. "I decree and declare that out of this pandemic shall rise the power of God in the outcast and the downtrodden of spirit, in the name of the Lord Jesus!"

Like a sleeper cell, read this book and rise to the call of God! Press into His power! Return and take your rightful place of authority. Wait to hear the voice of our Father. Then move in obedience to His Word. He still speaks even in the midst of the trials and tribulations of a pandemic. We have lost some battles, but the war has already been won. The blood of Christ has sealed our victory! Stay under the bloodstained banner and shout with a voice of victory while the battle is raging! Fight for the advancing kingdom and for the family of God in the earth!

Dare to step out and believe God!

CHAPTER 1

THE INTRODUCTION

THE POWER OF FORGIVENESS

The stench of unforgiveness fills the earth
like a never-ending stretch of landfills.
We the church have lost our posture
and position on the earth.
The Lord searches for the church as He
did in the days of the fall of humankind.
"Adam where are you?" (Genesis 3:9).
Our posture resembles the first Adam's
rather than that of the second Adam.
The first Adam blamed
God for sending Eve.
However, the second Adam
said, "Not my will; but, thine be
done" (Luke 22:42 KJV).
A lack of understanding and fear drove
the first Adam to cover himself.
But grace, mercy, and love were
in the second Adam and caused
Him to die for the first Adam.

The first Adam didn't understand leaves
are temporary and cannot hide sin.
The second Adam knew that only the
eternal blood of a perfect lamb could
take away the sins of the world.
It was the perfect plan of God for a
fallen world—past, present, and future!
The blood was shed by the second Adam
so we could be forgiven for our sins.
Yes, Jesus died, but before He died, He
said, "Father forgive them for they know
not what they do!" (Luke 23:34 KJV).
Forgiveness was released as an example
to all of us who are dying to self.
When we die, the church will
live! Resurrection power will
run through our veins!
God will be exalted, and the
stench of unforgiveness will
turn into a sacred aroma!
Let the sweet incense of worship be
released from the earth! God be glorified!
Forgiveness restores the church
and honors the second Adam.
Lord, as we forgive, we are forgiven
and your *power* is released.
Restore us, Lord, to the correct
posture and position of abundant life

in You! (*Soultry: Poetry from the Soul for the Soul!* by +D.L. Calhoun)

Soultry is a genre of prose that I created to express the heart of God on matters concerning life. It is a type of soi-disant stream of consciousness as given to me by the Holy Spirit. According to the *Oxford Dictionary*, soi-disant is a French word that simply means "self-styled." My pattern of soultry uniquely creates a subgenre of poetry. This particular work gives us access to the current state of the church. It elevates the prerequisites for the power of God to be released on the earth through the power of forgiveness. We often talk about forgiveness religiously. Case in point, forgiveness at its core can be a struggle for us, depending on the depth of the offense and our level of spiritual maturity. We forgive an offense, and that is human. However, to forget the offense is divine. We need God to help us complete or actualize this process in its entirety.

As we begin this book, we will need to examine areas of unrepented sin and look at our lives through the lens of God to determine our position in Him. Many of us think we are in a greater position or relationship with God than we actually are, according to God Himself. We boast about an anointing that belongs to Him. We tell people how good God is to us. We acknowledge how He is blessing us. Yet our spiritual lives look like the haunted house in the movies with the tattered curtains.

Our prayer life is less than adequate. Our study life has dwindled to a digital trickle or a daily scripture on the phone, which of course is better than nothing at all. Meanwhile, our church attendance has become an optional social sidebar.

We have become a religious mess, yet God still loves us and desires to have a relationship with us. He wants to release His power to us even though we are broken vessels. He has the power to make us whole again and to give us a perfected restoration. We have to acknowledge our brokenness before Him, dropping the weight of our facades. Pretending to be whole every Saturday or Sunday and Tuesday or Wednesday when we long to tell someone the truth. "Who can we trust?" we ask ourselves. The only person we can truly trust is God. We have to get back in the right position or posture with Him, and we will see His listening heart and His healing hand. "Love, grace, mercy, and forgiveness leak from His presence."

There is a running pattern in the Bible of Jesus forgiving people of their sins before He blesses them. We all need to be forgiven, and with the grace that God has given us, we need to learn how to forgive others. Forgiveness frees us to walk in a meaningful way with the Father. It demonstrates His love for us. It also helps us to build an intimate relationship with Him because there is nothing that we are too ashamed to bring to Him. Like Adam and Eve, in spite of our public personas and smooth facades, we are all naked before God, and we all need Him more than we are willing to admit. As we trust Him with our lives, He empowers us with more of His life flowing through us.

Don't underestimate the need for divine healing in order to release the power of God in your life. The converse of this grace toward us is the power of forgiveness through us releasing the power of God in the lives of others. This cycle of grace empowers the body of Christ to change the world. One man's forgiveness and sacrifice has brought billions to God through the resurrection power of the cross. Jesus said this prayer in Luke 23:34 (NKJV) while hanging on a cross that they put Him on: "Father, forgive them; for they do not know what they do."

THE FOCUS

However, that is not the main focus of this work. Soon I will release another book that focuses on this liberating aspect of the body of Christ we call forgiveness. The focus of this work is learning how to press through this present darkness into the light of the presence of Jesus Christ. Our goal is to walk in the resurrection power of Jesus Christ. Paul had a similar goal, and he wrote powerful words about it in Philippians 3:10 (NET), "My aim is to know him, to experience the power of his resurrection, to share in his sufferings, and to be like him in his death."

Before you get any deeper into this book, please know that it is not meant to be a get-rich guide or a manual for living your best life. This book is designed to set people free from the hidden bondages of life. It is also designed to debunk the myth that Christianity is for punks, because it is definitely not. To be a Christian or a believer in this era will take a lot of social grit and courage. It also encompasses us leaning on the eternal hands of God for everything, especially grace, mercy, and guidance.

I am compelled by God to give you a crash course in perseverance. In case you don't know it by now, Christianity is a commitment to God that you can walk away from at any time. However, as easy as that was to say, it is much harder to do once you have really given yourself to Christ. The next thing you need to know is that the promise of blessings is not synonymous with *MTV Cribs* or *Lifestyles of the Rich and Famous.* If that were the case, there would not be many Christians in the world.

I have traveled to many places around the world, and many believers live average, normal lives. On the other hand, many believers also live below what we would call the poverty line by American standards and love Jesus with all their hearts. They are content and blessed. I have worshipped with them on mountainsides in open-air churches, with animals coursing between our seats. The worship was pure and undefiled, yet people had very little in the way of material wealth. They have less, yet they have more. They are wealthy because of their love for God. In my travels, I learned a lot about dying to self. Paul had it right when he spoke about abounding and abasing. Do some believers get blessed with abundance? Sure they do. God has believers on all types of assignments in all arenas of life.

You just have to be willing to accept your specific assignment, whatever it might be, wherever it might be, and whenever you are called upon. Now, this assignment is not a one-size-fits-all garment. It is tailor-made for each of us based on our kingdom capacity and maturity. God gives us what we need to complete His work in the earth. We are all different, and we all have different gifts and varying spheres of influence. We are not to compare ourselves with others. Instead, we are required to come alongside one another and help one another get to the place God has ordained for our lives.

Each of us is a type of Simon of Cyrene. We are on the earth to help one another. More specifically, we are here to help bear one another's cross. We are our brother's keeper even in the midst of a spirit of selfishness that is more pervasive on the earth than ever before. Unfortunately, most of us operate under the guise of me, myself, and I. "What have you done for me lately?" "What is in it for me?" That is not the heart of the servant. Nor is that the heart of God! We are all ministers or servants of God and for one another on the earth. We are submitted one to another. We are called to assist one another and to edify one another for a greater vision and a greater purpose.

We only win together. We celebrate together. We are the joints that supply what each joint needs. We are to bear one another's burdens. We are assigned to pray for one another. We are designed to cooperate with one another as one body. We are under the sovereignty of one Lord, one faith, and one baptism. We may be separated by our different styles of worship, but at the end of the day, we are one church under the bloodstained banner of Jesus Christ.

United, we will be able to stand against the wiles of the enemy. However, divided we become victims of the very plot and deceit that Satan used on Adam and Eve against God. *Divide and conquer* is Satan's number one strategy against the body of Christ and the world. Look at the ravishing effects of racism in the world today! Once we are separated from God and one another, we become easy prey for the enemy. Similar to the stray or sick animal in a pack when leopards are hunting. Leopards always look for the easy catch. The one who is separated from the herd is always the easiest one to catch and devour. *Divide and conquer* was also deployed by Satan to orchestrate the first murder when Cain killed Abel. This was a breach of relationship and the direct domino effect of the fall of humankind. Lord, help us to open our eyes that we may see and identify the tricks of the enemy, in Jesus's name. Amen!

As we gather and emerge as one church, God will release a wave of resurrection power that only occurs when people come together for a divine and common cause. Expect a spiritual tsunami of epic proportions will invade the earth and cause people to come into the knowledge of the Lord Jesus Christ. The COVID-19 pandemic was one such tsunami. It leveled massive and sweeping changes to the faith. Many who were borderline or outside of the faith have renewed their relationship with God. The pandemic helped us to understand that life as we knew it could be altered with an errant cough or a sneeze. We lost loved ones unexpectantly. The socioeconomic landscape of the world changed within a matter of weeks.

However, there was one constant and immutable force in the world. It was the source of my sustainability during the pandemic, and it was God! I saw His visible hand. My Father was given approximately nine days to live. He had a plethora of underlying conditions. My sister and I were under flight restrictions, and my father could not have visitors. Besides, we were both approximately a thousand miles away from my father when he contracted COVID-19. The doctor's prognosis was bleak, and all we could do was pray and solicit the fervent prayers of the saints. Two weeks later, my father was cleared of any trace of COVID-19 at seventy-nine years of age. He was considered a prime target for its grim rampage. God is more than able!

Now, by no means if you lost a relative does that mean that God is not able. It speaks to the sovereign nature of God. The scripture declares in Hebrews 9:27, it is appointed to humankind to die, and after death, the judgment. In short, we all have an appointment with God. He alone determines how we transition from this life. When it is our time to transition, it is our time. Life and death are in the hands of the Father.

God is concerned about the life and activity of His children. His thoughts toward us are too innumerable to count (Psalm 139:17–18). In the wake of life's insurmountable impediments, we need to learn to trust in the will of God for our lives. Many of us have been bound and shackled by unhealthy relationships, toxic communications, or debilitating habits that almost killed us. God's Word intervenes in our daily lives, and we survived because "no weapon formed against us shall prosper" (Isaiah 54:17 NKJV). Case in point, the antitoxin has been released in His Word, and all we have to do is become true to our own selves. First, we have to examine ourselves to make sure we are in the faith (2 Corinthians 13:5 NKJV), especially while we are trying to build and help everyone else up in the faith. We will not be able to assist others until we ourselves have been made whole.

Sometimes we need to stop and check our spiritual compasses and see what the Lord is saying to us. Many of us have existed on what the Lord said past tense. We need to reset and sit quietly so we can hear what the Lord is saying to us now presently. Rule of thumb is that we follow the last instruction or command we received from God. Too many people are stuck in the negative grips of a former command, angry with God. We have literally been given new commands that we are unable to decipher because we are not on the same page with God.

Be honest with yourselves and ask the question, When is the last time we really heard from God? When is the last time we got a mandate to do a particular thing for God? Are we meandering in a quasi-Christian space, hiding out or hanging out in a ministry that we used to be called to, but we are afraid to do something different? I am not necessarily talking about an audible voice coming from heaven, although God can speak like that if He so chooses. I am really referring to praying and reading God's Word until transformation comes as a result of this divine inoculation and interaction with the will and presence of God Almighty!

Hence, when our pastors speak on Sundays, Tuesdays, and Wednesdays, we should be receiving a word of confirmation that lets us know we are in tune with the Father. This should not be the first time we have heard from God all week or, worse than that, all month. Let's explore some prohibitions to our relationship with God.

Remember, this is a private examination of self. No one is in the room except you and God. Let the Holy Spirit work through you to examine the possibilities.

Why live beneath your privilege in terms of your relationship with God? I received Christ wanting to live an abundant life. I have learned through trial and error that it is easy to lose your way. It is so easy to stray off the path. Life presents a myriad of detours that will engage you. However, grace will always allow you the means and opportunity to find your path back to God. There is no one-size-fits-all concerning our relationship with God. You and the Holy Spirit chart your own course based on the specific will of God for your life. The key is relinquishing the power of the flesh to the Holy Spirit and keeping that as the baseline for our Christian walk. The Holy Spirit will never steer us wrong. His goal is to please the Father by leading and guiding us to all truth and understanding. Are you ready now? It's time to learn how to recognize and shed demonic strongholds in our lives. It is time for us to gain an understanding of what it means to press into His power. I will close this chapter with a few verses of scripture that have helped me during my Christian journey. They are found in 1 John 1:5–10 NLT:

> This is the message we heard from Jesus and now declare to you: God is light, and there is no darkness in Him at all. So we

are lying if we say we have fellowship with God but go on living in spiritual darkness; we are not practicing the truth. But if we are living in the light, as God is in the light, then we have fellowship with each other, and the blood of Jesus, His Son, cleanses us from all sin. If we claim we have no sin, we are only fooling ourselves and not living in the truth. But if we confess our sins to Him, He is faithful and just to forgive us our sins and to cleanse us from all wickedness. If we claim we have not sinned, we are calling God a liar and showing that His word has no place in our hearts.

SECTION II

FAITH AND TECHNOLOGY

CHAPTER 2

FAITH

THE NECESSITY OF THE FAITH

Contrary to popular opinion or what might even be considered politically correct, Christianity is not some magical or imaginary ascent to God. Instead, there are stages of growth and development—rigorous test of character, faith, and longsuffering that vary from individual to individual based on your God-given capacity. When I say capacity, I refer to your capacity to endure the tests inherent with the faith. This is no cakewalk, and this is definitely not for chumps who need "magic wand faith" or immediate results, although Christianity may be able to provide practical steps to achieving life goals. Those steps are in the introduction to the faith at the very tip of an iceberg of instruction and guidance.

I have been in the faith for nearly forty years. I have gone through a series of high and lows and my own personal triumphs and tragedies. I have gotten to know God on many levels. In my infant years of the faith, He carried me through very polemical or difficult situations.

In my later years, He became the God who informed me that I am old enough to walk through the fire without being carried. He has been the God who shields me and the God who says, "These things must come to pass. Now endure hardness as a good soldier of Jesus Christ." I have laughed, and I have cried. I have been settled and sure and blind and baffled. I have been surrounded by people and alone simultaneously. I have been at the top of my game professionally—then thrust to the bottom to start all over again, having to reinvent myself in Christ.

Better communicated, there were times when I knew exactly who I was in Christ and then times when I asked the Lord, "Where am I going? Who am I, and what do you want me to do now?" True Christianity is a toss between riding on a Ferris wheel and riding on the Hulk roller coaster. More than not, it's like Disney's Space Mountain, because you can't see anything until you get there and it is time to board the ride. Other times, it is like the smooth DMV transit system versus the ride-at-your-own-risk NYC transit system. Christianity cannot be cloned and is never predictable. Although you will experience pockets of happiness in the faith, that is not the goal of Christianity. Our goal is to learn how to be obedient to God's will, no matter the cost.

As I read the narrative of Jesus in the Gospels, He is constantly under attack. Jesus was bombarded by the cares of the people who had an insatiable appetite to be in His presence. Nevertheless, they practiced abstinence concerning the idea of practicing what He taught. The religious leadership of His day shunned Him for the most part and considered Him a threat to the established religious order. Circumstances of this nature, coupled with the fact that His ultimate outcome was to be the sacrificial lamb for the sins of the world, left very little room for happiness.

Now I am not saying that God never wants us to be happy. There will be points and times of happiness in your walk with God, but the lack thereof cannot be a sign to you that God is not with you. He is always with us. In fact, whether you are happy, sad, depressed, confused, or any other emotional state you can think of, our faith guarantees the presence of God. Knowing that He is there is a matter of faith and relationship with Him. God will be there to give you what you need to fulfill His will for your life. He is our very present help in the time of trouble (Psalm 46:1 KJV). He has the ability to bring you great joy during very trying times.

His joy will sustain you and give you strength (Nehemiah 8:10 NKJV). The life of Jesus was anything but the pursuit of happiness or living His best life. He was in pursuit of the will of God! That should be the aim of every believer in Christ. Paul, one of the most prolific writers in the New Testament, spoke about this very same thing in no uncertain terms to the church at Corinth. Here is a quote found in 2 Corinthians 5:9–10 (NKJV): "Therefore we make it our aim, whether present or absent, to be well pleasing to Him. For we must all appear before the judgment seat of Christ, that each one may receive the things done in the body, according to what he has done, whether good or bad."

The goal of the faith is not just to be saved or born again. This starts the process and begins the journey that we call salvation. The goal of the faith is not just to join a church, then a ministry, and to become obedient to the will of God through the teaching and preaching of the faith. The goal of the faith is not just to shout, dance, speak in tongues, and get a prophetic word while experiencing the charismatic power of God. Nor is the goal to rise up in the spiritual ranks from a fledging pew dweller to an influential and well-recognized pastor.

None of the aforementioned things are bad, negative, or wrong. In fact, I pray that you get the opportunity to experience the fullness of our faith. I have been there, done that and embraced all of these transitions in my life. They were good times in the faith, but there is more, and there is life after pastoring and preaching. However, that is another book. We must understand that the ways of God are beyond our comprehension, and His plan beyond the scope of our thinking.

Christianity in its purest sense is primarily about the pursuit of God. It is secondarily learning to harness the power of God in you through the power of the Holy Spirit. Christianity should not be limited to a Sunday, Tuesday, or Wednesday experience. It is a way of life.

This is not just reading the Bible but understanding the traditions, customs, and culture of the Bible. This understanding will make it possible for us to translate and apply it to our lifestyles in any era of life. Christianity requires us to live with Christ daily, and we cannot turn this on and off like a light switch. We press in every day to make application of what we have read and heard to live a life that glorifies God.

In preaching, we study the Word to try to help believers better understand the Bible so they can live a godly life. We call this a hermeneutical transfer, taking biblical times and learning how to make application for today's society without changing the original intent. Hermeneutics is the science of biblical interpretation. I am not trying to drop you off at the nearest seminary between the divine and the academic. However, I do want us to be clear on the objective of our faith. Our focus in life should be learning the importance of understanding the Word of God and the role it plays in our daily lives.

Developing this understanding and converting it to wisdom is a lifelong pursuit. The point I am trying to make is that true Christianity will cause you to die to yourself, and this is not always a happy place but a place that you will have to evolve to understand. Dying to one's self is not an option in the faith. It is the ultimate goal, and it is not easy. In fact, it is something you will be doing all your life. We become powerless so we can press into His power. Read 2 Corinthians 12:9 (NKJV).

In our weakness, the power of God will be made strong because of the grace of God that covers His children. In short, you will know God is with you when you are in your weakest and most vulnerable times. I have discovered having nowhere else to turn is a good place. This is the lesson we will learn from the paralytic man later in the book.

CHAPTER 3

THE INTERSECT

THE INTERSECTION OF FAITH AND TECHNOLOGY

Time is the intersect between faith and technology. By intersect, I mean the core ingredient necessary for the development of our faith and the use of the internet. Time is a critical component of both. Thus, the stewardship of time takes years to master. On the other hand, time is highly sought after by the devil as well. The enemy looks to steal time and corrupt our stewardship of time by any means necessary. He knew that if he spent enough time talking to Eve, eventually she and Adam would succumb to his wicked scheme. Think about it. The lust of the flesh, the lust of the eyes, and the pride of life are all produced over a period of time by giving the person increasing periods of exposure to the thing or things they desire.

Adam and Eve had to be standing in front of the Tree of Life while Satan tricked them using the power of suggestion. The serpent was smooth and subtle. Listen to his words. Then the serpent said to the woman, "You will not surely die" (Genesis 3:4 ESV). In Genesis 1:1–7 (NKJV), Satan weaves a masterful web using the power of words to create a picture of being like God. The algorithms used in the technology of the internet have this system or protocol down to perfection. It analyzes our web searches and puts these objects in front of us all day, giving us increased exposure to things we may like but don't need. Take a quick look at James 1:14–15 (NET): "But each one is tempted when he is lured and enticed by his own desires. Then when desire conceives, it gives birth to sin, and when sin is full grown, it gives birth to death." The scripture confirms the process by which sin gets into our hearts. Prolonged exposure will capture your mind and heart. How long can you play with fire before you get burned? Time should be treasured and used wisely. Moreover, what we do with time should be filtered by our faith.

As you can tell by the previous discourse, Christianity takes a lot of time to master and should therefore be protected. Thus, I coined another phrase that I have been teaching for years, "Time is the most valuable commodity in the world." It can only be redeemed and controlled by God Himself. Time is not subject to humankind. Even when we try to utilize Ephesians 5:16 (NKJV), we have to entreat the throne of grace. Humans cannot redeem time without the express consent and direction of God. Hezekiah did not give himself an additional fifteen years. God did! It was the will of the

Father. From the very beginning of time, in Genesis 1, we were given the divine demonstration about the significance of time.

First, God created light and separated it from the darkness, thus creating what we now call night and day. Night and day were the first elements of time. This distinction is not necessary for God. However, it is necessary for us. Night and day are indiscriminate to God. Psalm 139:12 (NKJV) states, "Indeed, the darkness shall not hide from You, but, the night shines as day; the darkness and the light are both alike to You." Thus, God created light for us, and light was the central necessity added to darkness to create a workday—time set aside for us to be productive. This was the first day of seven days, and six of them were created for working, while one day was specifically created to rest. On the fourth day, in Genesis 1:14–19 (NKJV), it is clear that God is setting up "signs, seasons, days and years." Hence, time was being established in the earth in such a way that it would perpetually affect humanity until time yielded to eternity. In other words, we would live and base our days and appointments around the sequence of time.

God teaches us several lessons in Genesis. These lessons are critical to our current understanding of the use of time. There are two variables that must be considered; one is called process, and the other is referred to as protocol. God is sovereign and all-powerful. He could have negated the use of time and voided the six-day use of process and protocol. In fact, He could have created the world, the universe, and all existence in the vacuum of His thoughts or in less time than it would take to blink an eye or to snap a finger like Thanos. However, He introduces us to Himself as the God who values the time necessary to create processes, protocols, scope, sequence, planning, self-inspection, evaluation, and excellence. Moreover, God completely avoids haste; He demonstrates a patience that shows humanity the importance of time management.

God's use of time management in the book of Genesis clearly introduces us to these two variables. The first one is process. By illustration, God creates the world using process. Everything in life has a process. There is nothing created and living in the earth that does not have a process. Building and developing anything of substance takes time. Excellence is the objective of proper time management. Excellence as a standard for productivity always adds value to the final outcome.

For example, I have personally edited this book extensively. I wanted my thoughts to be clear and concise. Editing is a meticulous and painstaking process that consumes inordinate amounts of time. It is usually repeated too many times to count—repetitive writing and rewriting again and again. This often meant pushing back deadlines to create an environment of excellence. The goal was simple. I wanted this book to be written in excellence, and I wanted you, the reader, to be blessed.

When the reader is blessed, God gets the glory! So, I could not rush the process to create the final product. I had to take time to add value in order to produce an excellent literary work.

The second variable is protocol or the consistent parameters or systems used in creation to speak certain things into existence. Protocols also explore the parameters or systems used to make humanity by hand out of things that were already in existence. If you read Genesis very carefully, you will see that some things were spoken into existence while others were hand fashioned by God Himself. He followed a series of protocols to create and to make everything, and these protocols are still perpetual to this day. Simply stated, God teaches us the life lesson that we should establish and apply systems or protocols to our daily lives. Some of these protocols are inherent in the transference of our DNA, while other protocols are passed on through family legacy. Protocols are the basis for generational sustainability.

My parents had protocols concerning my sister and me. Since I am six years older than my sister, I will speak from my vantage point. When I came home from elementary school, I had to remove my school clothes and immediately start my homework. I changed because we did not have a lot of money and I had to take care of the clothes I had. After or during the homework process, my mother would give me a snack. After eating the snack, I would sometimes do extra math. I had to read to her out loud every day. She expected me to pause at commas, stop at periods, and to show excitement if there was an exclamation point. I would get so angry, and tears would stream down my face. I wanted to go outside and play with my friends. She said with emphasis, "Boy! I am trying to help you be something someday." She was teaching me how to press in, and I was too young to understand. These protocols aided me in my personal development and in my relationship with God.

In life, there are certain things you have to develop, such as routines, schedules, or protocols, in order to be productive. We cannot fly by night with our eyes closed and expect the best. Routines, like anything in life, require discipline. There is a certain amount of discipline required to pursue a long-term relationship with God. There will be times when you have to press in to His presence to obtain His power. We all encounter this passion of pursuit in different ways, but it is hardwired into our human DNA. During this process, I was prone to self-sabotage, which will always result in either delay or demise. As a result, I wanted to stop reading, and I wanted out of my mother's regiment.

Nevertheless, she knew it would produce an excellent outcome, and she had a fierce determination that outweighed my attitude and my tears. My mother's influence and grit helped me to get over the hurdle of self. In order to break out of the shackles of your past and change your present plight in life, you are going to have to put up a fight. It is two in the morning, but I will not stop until God gets the glory. I am pressing in. I am on a theological dissertation committee, and I have a 5:00 a.m. conference call. My mind says to sleep, but my Spirit says, "Write." The Spirit will defeat the flesh, but we have a role as well. We must fight our old nature to cooperate with God's will for our lives. We have to press in! No matter what the obstacles are that stand in front of us!

I need to spend some serious time developing and expanding my thoughts in the next few paragraphs, but for now, let me just walk us through some insights that mesh with pressing into His power. Before I move on, let me quickly summarize my previous thoughts in these words: *Time is the child of eternity. It produces the will of God. Process is the natural patterns of time and growth necessary to develop maturity. Protocols are the systems, procedures, steps, and safeguards that ensure proper development and sustainability of that growth and maturity.*

As this chapter concludes, here are some genuine points of interest. I do not care what station you are in in life. I declare that if you are breathing, God is not through with you yet. If you are in prison reading this book, you may have a confined lifestyle, but your spirit self can be free to roam the universe in God. The gospel is not chained or bound. (2 Timothy 2:9) God can use you regardless of what you have done. You m living in the ashes of past mistakes, and God can still use you. Divorced, an ex-this and ex-that, God can still use you. God is not limited by our past performances or the deficiencies of our personal résumés.

In fact, here is some insight taken from Jeremiah 29:11 (NKJV). God has a plan for all of our lives to give us a future and a hope. Moreover, He has calculated all possible outcomes to know exactly where we would be today, mentally, physically, emotionally, and spiritually. He has given time permission to wait on us to come to this place in life and then to release new possibilities, because today is unlike any other day.

We have finally arrived at the place where we are ready to give life and God a chance again. We are ready to press in to His presence. We are ready to ignore all of the weights of our past. We are ready to acknowledge that He alone is God and there is no one like Him. We finally understand that there is no one above Him or below Him who can change us but Him. Time, process, and protocol have brought us to this place of maturation and brokenness that makes us the perfect candidate for fighting to get in the presence and power of God. We are finally ready to take on this unseen challenge of life. Like the paralytic we will read about later, we are ready to overcome whatever has been holding us back.

We have nothing else to lose but our lives. Jacob could not beat the angel, but he said, "I will not let you go unless you bless me" (Genesis 32:26 NKJV). We need to learn to fight for what belongs to us. Just because God promises us something does not mean we will get it without a fight. The fight will require an understanding of three things. Yes, you guessed it. Watch this: time, process, and protocol. Look at the children of Israel in the book of Joshua. They had to fight for the possession of the promised land, and it did not just fall in their laps overnight.

Ask George Washington Carver, Thomas Edison, Garrett Morgan, Alexander Graham Bell, Margaret Knight, the Wright brothers, Marie Van Brittan Brown, Lewis Howard Latimer, and Patricia Bath about the importance of time, process, and protocols. All of these men and women went through a series of failures in order to develop the processes and protocols for success. Every major inventor, builder, scientist, professional athlete, and world-class performer in any creative art understands the importance of time. Without time, none of the aforementioned men and women would have changed the world as we know it today. God created time for us. Thus, God took seven days to create something He could have created in seconds or less to teach us the value of time.

Time allows gestation periods to bring God's creation from a seed form to maturity, like a California redwood tree (approximately sixty-five years), or from a draft on a blueprint to the world's tallest single standing building, Burj Khalifa in Dubai. It took six years to build. Listen carefully. The genesis of the construction of a building starts with a thought or concept. This thought could have been in the mind of the builder for years—maybe even since he was a small child. However, processes like this one have been in the mind of God since the beginning of time. It had to be in the mind of God first. Then God transferred it into the existence of the head and heart of a man. This process occurred long before it was ever put on paper as a concept drawing—well before it became a blueprint, approved by business and governmental authorities and financed by banks and venture capitalists. It took time. So hang in there! Keep reading. It has always been just a matter of time! Remember, God has your future on His mind right now. Prepare to fight for your future!

CHAPTER 4

TECHNOLOGY

TIME AND TECHNOLOGY

By now, I hope you understand that our faith and technology have a mutual and strategic intersect that the enemy understands extremely well. It is called time. Listen to the *Oxford* definition of time in its verb form. Time is "to plan, schedule or arrange when (something) should happen or be done." In this light, God is the master of time. Before I proceed, I want you to know that I am sensitive to the digital culture that many of you have grown up in. I am well aware of the natural inclinations of my audience. So, let me pause and state that I am by no means antitechnology. Nor am I against digital platforms that make it easier for us to communicate and live in this postmodern era. I just want us to utilize technology with the wisdom of God. *We must learn to control it and harness its power rather than letting it control us and harness our power.*

As we move forward in our text, we must clearly understand the importance of time, especially in the role it plays concerning pressing into the presence of God.

For example, I have an Instagram presence. In order to write this book, I had to shut it off for several weeks because of its time-capturing nature. Like all forms of social media, it must be monitored for time usage. I have discovered that people spend more time on social media platforms in a week than they spend with God in an entire month. Anything that grabs our attention like that can be considered an idol. An idol is anything that separates us from the love of God. You see, whatever we love the most will get the bulk of our time and energy.

We need to recognize time stealers. Let's keep it real. Digital platforms can be used to communicate truth, to share memories, to commemorate people or special days. It can also be used for productivity like business and marketing. Unfortunately, it can also be used to promote mindless activities that send us down the rabbit holes of someone else's life. Case in point, if we just spent an hour or two doing absolutely nothing positive on social media, how do we make the claim that we do not have enough time to complete tasks in life that have relevance and meaning? People say they don't have time to do some of the things that will transform their lives for the better—things that could produce income, a new career path, or just an overall trajectory for a better quality of life. We would rather spend time writing comments to posts we either like or hate. Sometimes this erupts into a series of exhaustive arguments with people you will never meet, who hide behind a digital moniker or alias.

However, this exercise or routine—generally speaking—adds little or no value to the context of your life.

The internet boasts a plethora of time-stealing activities, from video games and shopping to pornography, challenges, crude humor, heresy, and the rants of ignorant or amoral people who don't have a clue about life. There are all sorts of things that can consume inordinate amounts of time if watched in excess. The enemy's other attack is using subtle suggestions based on our previous search algorithms to divert our attention from productivity to busyness. Being productive and being busy are two different things. Busyness is simply the task of being occupied doing something or anything. Being busy does not equate to productivity. Being productive is the act of intentionally working on a task for a specific and desired outcome. We cannot allow the enemy to steal our time using the internet.

According to Broadband Search, the average person in the world spends 144 minutes a day on social media or two hours and twenty-four minutes. Multiply that by seven days a week, and we come up with 1,008 minutes or 16.8 hours a week. That is easily the equivalent of working a part-time job. Generally speaking, people don't like to spend two cumulative hours with God all week. I pastored for twenty years. Moreover, wherever I lived over the past forty years, I would make it my business to be involved with a local church. In my tenure as a pastor and parishioner, I observed people who could not pray for more than two minutes in a single prayer setting or pay attention for more than five minutes.

If we continue on this trajectory as a people, eventually we will spend more time on the internet than we do pursuing the things that improve our quality of life. Spending time with God in prayer and the study of His Word gives our life meaning and direction. Secondly, we will miss the will of God for our lives because we are buried in internet minutiae. We will be trapped in the trivial pursuit of trying to keep up with other people and the constantly changing culture of this world.

When do we spend time with our children, our spouse, and our families? When do we write books and business plans? When do we have time to learn investment strategies? When do we have time to exercise or to learn how to cook healthier? When do we have time to complete our vision boards or go back to school? When do we develop meaningful relationships and interpersonal communication skills? When do we have time to go to church? When will we have time to read the Word, which activates our purpose in life, or even to develop a meaningful and deliberate prayer time? When do we have time to hear God download information pertaining to solutions for world problems or our purpose in the world? When will we have time to cultivate a significant relationship with God so we can learn to press into His power? There is a lot of productivity that can fit into 16.8 hours per week. When will we make time to press into the power of God?

One of the things I pray that each of us has to be intentional about is examining our lives for time stealers. Anything that takes inordinate amounts of time from our flow of productivity can be causing us to lose vital territory in the kingdom. Take the time to examine your time management. Prioritize the things that are important. Make sure God is at the top of your list of priorities! Nothing in your life should have a greater commitment than the things God is holding you accountable to be a steward over. Then begin to build a schedule that accentuates divine productivity over wasted and unaccountable spaces of time. Wasting time always leads to critical lapses in judgment. Instead, be sure to build in time for the preparation and processes that will cause you to want to press into the power in order to fulfill your purpose on earth.

SECTION III

THE FIGHT, THE PRESS, AND THE VICTORY

CHAPTER 5

THE FIGHT

FIGHTING THE ADDICTIONS OF THE PAST

Generally speaking, Christians often enter spiritual gun fights with a knife mentality. We underestimate both of the major players in the fight, and then we are overconfident in our own abilities. The first major player is in the blue corner, wearing a purple and gold robe, riding on a white horse with a two-edged sword, representing the Truth and Eternal Boxing Team, our champion, Jesus, always known as (a.k.a.) the Prince of Peace. He is the undefeated and undisputed Sovereign Champion of Eternity, past, present, and future. His opponent, the next major player, in the black corner, wearing black on black, being carried by a legion of imps, representing the Kingdom of Darkness and Spiritual Wickedness in High Places Team is the contender, Satan, always known as (a.k.a.) the prince of the air. He is the reigning world champion.

They will battle for the prize of humanity. God loves and created humanity in His own image. Humanity must decide, using free will, who they are going to support in this fierce battle. Will they support Team Eternity or Team Darkness? If humanity goes with Jesus, they must learn to have no confidence in the arm of the flesh. On the other hand, they can support Team Darkness, who promises them that they can live their best life now void of Christ and the church. We come into this world with a slight handicap because we were born and shaped in iniquity (Psalm 51:5 NKJV). Moreover, because we were born in the earth realm, we have an affinity for or an addiction to things of the flesh. That addiction embraces the things we can see, touch, and smell.

As members of humanity, we are overwhelmed by the influences of the material world in our lives. Like Adam and Eve, we are attracted to the lust of the flesh, the lust of the eyes, and the pride of life. According to 1 John 2:16 (NKJV), these things come from the world and not God. The lust of the flesh is the over pursuit or the love of things. This list of things can include but is not limited to the following: food, sports, drugs, sex, sexual perversions, alcohol, smoking, sugar, pornography, TV, social media, movies, binging, people, toxic relationships, money, laziness, control, video games, adrenaline rushes, underachieving, or anything your body can become chemically, anatomically, emotionally, or psychologically addicted to.

The lust of the eyes is a serious attraction to anything you see and desire. It can be clothes, a man or woman married or single, the lifestyle of the rich and famous, art, shoe fetishes, nails, hair, sneakers, designer clothes, luxury, or fast cars. It can be the pursuit of something that satisfies your need to compete with the Joneses, based on the prescribed fads, culture, or preferences of the world. The lust of the eyes is a doorway to sin that is the equivalent to opening Pandora's box. In Greek mythology, Pandora was the first woman in the earth. She was both beautiful and curious. Although she was instructed by the gods not to open the box, she opened the box anyway and unleashed all of the social ills of the world. Now, I do not subscribe to Greek mythology, but the point of this didactic myth is clear. In short, do not sleep or let your guards down concerning the lust of the eyes. It can lead to a host of other sins like envy, stealing, lying, covetousness, adultery, or jealousy.

The pride of life can come in a variety of attributes or characteristics. The pride of life is the driving force or the love for things like positions, titles, education, associations, the need to be liked by people, recognition, status, being in charge or out front, attention seeking, power, prestige, acclaim, fame, authority, cliques, overachieving or the necessity to feel needed, racism, and ethnic pride. The pride of life is anything that allows you to brag about who you are, what you do, or what you are pretending to be. The pride of life makes people feel better about themselves. Simultaneously, they shun or belittle people who are not a part of their inner circle, clique, organization, or status group.

The pride of life robs people of the place reserved for God's presence and humility. It is humility that captures the attention and affections of God. Meekness is the twin of humility. Meekness is the ability to have authority yet to be subject to authority or under authority. Meekness is the ability to have power and not flaunt it. Jesus was meek. Jesus was able to possess absolute power and to control it for the greater good of the kingdom of God. Without humility and meekness, He would have never given His life for the sins of humanity.

Humility and meekness add value to the lives of other people. They are the exact opposites of the pride of life, which is all about self-gratification and public demonstrations of false humility. False humility is the act of helping people with the intent of being seen or drawing attention to yourself while having an ulterior motive for your display of kindness. False humility draws God's contempt, not His blessing. God knows the thoughts and intents of our hearts (Hebrews 4:12 KJV). Take a quick look at Jeremiah 17:10 NLT, "But I, the LORD, search all hearts and examine secret motives. I give all people their due rewards, according to what their actions deserve."

People who suffer from the pride of life often display attributes of being superior or better than other people or ethnic groups. The pride of life is the most divisive of the three addictive behaviors and can often be associated with delusions of grandeur. The blog entitled Goodtherapy.org has a great definition of delusions of grandeur: "A delusion of grandeur is the false belief in one's own superiority, greatness, or intelligence. People experiencing delusions of grandeur do not just have high self-esteem; instead, they believe in their own greatness and importance even in the face of overwhelming evidence to the contrary." Have you ever met someone who is pompous or self-important? They want you to be subject to their false sense of power, when we all should be subject to God and the authority of God alone. Does this mean that we listen to no one in authority? No, there are designated people in authority, because God put them in their place of position. However, no one in authority should endeavor to take the place of God. If they do, that is the spirit of the pride of life.

Yes, some of these categories or subtopics are interchangeable, and that is precisely what makes them so dangerous. They can be interwoven in the fabric of our daily lives and hidden in the posture of what we refer to as normal. They can be cloaked in these famous expressions: "That's just the way that I am," "I don't mean any harm," "I am not bothering anybody," "What's wrong with that?" Well, for starters, anything done in excess can be sin, especially if it consumes large amounts of your time or thinking process. We must always remember that God has a plan and a purpose for our lives. The enemy wearing the black trunks will do anything to stop or squelch this plan of God for your life.

Hence, the story of Adam and Eve or the fall of humankind found in Genesis, chapter 3. Satan has a very simple plan to come between God and humankind. He needs humans to cooperate with his subtle deconstruction of God's will. He strategically used deflective questions like the one found in verse 1, "Has God indeed said, 'You shall not eat of every tree of the garden'?" (Genesis 3:1 KJV). Without going into grave detail, Satan finds the weakness in Eve's armor when she alludes to the fact that touching the fruit will cause them to die. God never said that touching the fruit will cause you to die. So if Satan can get her to touch it and she does not die, the rest is history. In verses 5 and 6, he immediately challenges and opens the door for the pride of life, the lust of the flesh, and the lust of the eyes.

You know the rest of the story. Adam and Eve succumbed to the tricks of the devil, and for a season they lost their connection with God. Satan effectively stole their divine productivity because they were now preoccupied with the disastrous outcomes of sin. Hence, Satan interrupted their heavenly assignment. He stole enough time to take their attention off of the will of God. He lured them into a trap, using subtle questions, interjections, and suggestions, and got both of them to commit to going against the will of God for their lives. It was the perfect storm.

In closing, nothing is new under the sun. The enemy still uses some of the same tools of deception, especially if it is stealing time from what I call divine productivity. Divine productivity is the thing or things that we are supposed to be doing for God as part of our assignment on earth. God works through humanity through the power of the Holy Spirit to spread His love on earth. These are the things that please God, because they were commissioned by God. Divine productivity will bless your life on earth and in heaven.

For some people, because of the combination of one, two, or all three of these lusts or pride, people are blinded to the will of God for their lives. Therefore, they never achieve any semblance of divine productivity. Missing out on God's original intent and being trapped in a maze of sin is the enemy's plan for your life. Do not let him succeed. Get the victory over addiction by first being honest with yourself. Then turn to God with a heart of confession, repentance, and humility. Let God set you free from the bondages of addiction and celebrate His victory in your life. We can live a victorious life in Christ Jesus when we press into the power of God! The devil is a liar! Your life can change! Trust God for the victory over addiction that has already been won through Christ Jesus our Lord!

CHAPTER 6

THE PRESS AND THE VICTORY

PRESSING FOR THE VICTORY

Now, I do not want to suggest to you that defeating addictions are as easy as one, two, three, presto, and done. No it is a press, a struggle of will, determination, prayer, and reliance on God's mercy, forgiveness, and love. Daily, you have to fight the thoughts that flood your heart and mind, and then you have to resist the temptations of the devil. Each day will present its own test, and you should take it day by day. In the last chapter, I spoke about the lust of the flesh and eyes and the pride of life as formidable foes. The problem with these three ancient bedfellows is that once we submit to them, the desire or thirst for them can easily outweigh our hunger and thirst for God. Moreover, pride and lusts can come in combination packages that then lead its prey to a certain or inevitable downward spiral. These three often vie to occupy the throne of our hearts and can subtly, over time, become the object of our worship.

They are relentless in their pursuit of our focus. The lust of the flesh, the lust of the eyes, and the pride of life are insatiable.

In other words, they can never be satisfied. Since they can't be satisfied, they become dangerous addictive behaviors. These addictions or negative habits can go unchecked or undetected for years unless they are exposed by the Word of God. These habitual chains can only be broken through prayer and repentance and the power of God. Counseling and other measures of accountability can also be added to stem the tide of allowing these behaviors to reemerge. Your pastor, spouse, best friend, accountability partner, or counselor should also be a partner in this fight, helping you continue your journey to the fulfillment of your kingdom assignment on earth.

Addictions are not to be played with. They are kin to fire, and you will get burned. We have to press into God's power to overcome them. They cannot be ignored because they are hindrances to the presence and power of God. They steal time and damage relationships. These negative behaviors especially attack areas of our productivity, legacy, and people interactions, but more importantly, they interrupt our intimacy and worship with God. They have to be faced head-on. You must possess a made-up mind and the heart that you will not stop until you encounter the yoke-breaking anointing of God. Like the paralytic man of the Gospel of Mark and Luke, you cannot accept any excuses. We must get into the presence of God by any means necessary, even if it means exposing our weaknesses and getting help to accomplish the will of God for our life. The paralytic had the support of a team. He was helpless and hapless. Everybody knew it, and they thought he was wasting his time. I can hear them now. "Stop wasting time. Jesus does not want to see you!" Quite the contrary; not only does Jesus want to see us, but He radically wants to change our lives!

Writing this book has caused me to enlist the help of family and friends. I needed constant prayer support, encouragement from friends and family who rallied around my assignment and helped carry my bed. It has caused me to fight through my own personal demons, addictive behaviors, and the constant attacks of the enemy. I needed the power of God to help me to multitask family, writing, business, ministry, counseling, and clearing the clutters of life off my plate while pursuing my destiny and purpose in Christ. The clutter of life is all the unnecessary things that occupy space in our minds and hearts that may need to get done eventually, but right now in this moment, it is not necessary to complete them. Clutter causes you to push off priorities because it creates the feeling of being overwhelmed. You begin avoiding your priorities and putting them off till next week and next month. Unfortunately, next week and next month never come, and you find yourself in a valley of dry bones in the middle of your project or assignment. Get up and believe God in spite of your negative headspace, and press into the power of God.

I have spent countless hours writing, rewriting, editing, and toiling in prayer. Like David, I also had to learn how to encourage myself and speak life when I was overwhelmed with fear and the feelings of inadequacy. I had to press through fatigue, weariness, doubt, and discouragement while keeping my eyes focused on the light at the end of the tunnel. However, I was clear that unless I continued to press into the power of God, I would never be able to accomplish God's will for my life. He had to write through me. I had to become like an instrument ready to be played at all hours of the night and day. Many sacrifices of family time, sleep, leisure, and other personal and community obligations had to be put on the backburner to complete this project. I had to shut out all dissenting and contrary voices to the will of God for my life, remembering that not every good thing was a God thing for me in that season. You have to be clear on two things: first your assignment, and second, the purposes of God for your life. God had me writing in the middle of a pandemic, but this was my destiny and journey.

Furthermore, I had to stay focused and obedient to His voice. Opposition arose from many areas of my life. As I mentioned in the opening chapter my father contracted COVID-19. He was literally given a death sentence by his attending physician. At almost eighty years of age and more than one thousand miles away from my sister and me. In addition to that, we had travel and visiting restrictions in both the hospital and nursing homes that he was in and out of over a six- to eight-week period. Long-term care and home care are extremely expensive endeavors, and they take hours of phone interactions, research, and resource paperwork to put together a program that is tailored to meet the needs of your loved ones and your budget. God used my sister and my wife to get me through this season and to help me balance my kingdom productivity and responsibility to my father. They both had to be done at the same time, and I needed a team to help carry my bed.

After getting over that hurdle, my wife, two daughters, and I all got COVID-19 at the same time. I was in the middle of final edits when that COVID brain fog hit me. I was literally unable to read and comprehend my own book. Most of the days were spent in a delusional state, barely able to function. Somehow my wife took care of both of us, providing twenty-four-hour care. It was the power of God and a loving village of friends, relatives, and medical personnel that nursed me back to health from my home. I was out of commission for well over a month, and it took me two more months to get back on track. God's grace and His power will overcome all things. (I want to send special prayers out to the families who lost loved ones and continued health to the COVID survivors.)

The bottom line is you will never get the victory in anything in life that God has called you to do without facing life's obstacles and your fears and inhibitions. Then you have to examine your lifestyle and resolve to fight and eliminate any hindering habits or sins that keep you from accomplishing God's will for your life. You will need to look inward first to the power of the Holy Spirit. As born-again believers, we must recognize and acknowledge the gift of God given to us. Let me illustrate. First John 4:4 (KJV) states, "Ye are of God, little children, and have overcome them: because greater is He that is in you, than he that is in the world." The God of Abraham, Isaac, and Jacob in us is greater and more powerful than the god of this world outside of us.

We have to understand who we are as it relates to the kingdom of God on earth. Having a spiritual identity crisis is both dangerous and detrimental. No one should want to embrace being a spiritual orphan or nomad. That is why we study the Word of God. It helps us discover God's plan for our life and to find our identity in Christ. As the scripture declares through Peter, God, through His divine power, has given us everything that pertains to life and godliness (2 Peter 1:3). We have been given power over the spirits of this world. Christ has given us the ability to overcome the world. We overcome by the blood of the Lamb and the words of our testimony (Revelation 12:11).

This book is my testimony to the power of God.

His will is sovereign. It has been a long time coming. I have been writing for years, ever since my days in high school and especially during my matriculation through the English curriculum at Howard University. I have always known He wanted me to write, and I knew I had a gift of writing. However, there is no way to write or to do anything for God without entering a fight against the spiritual adversaries of this world. Pastor Dexter Upshaw and I self-published a coffee table book a few years back, and it took a lot of work, but the times were different, and I believe the impact of this book will be different. I really had to press into the power of God to complete this one. Paul kept it real and "one hundred" when he said where there are open and effectual doors, there are many adversaries (1 Corinthians 16:9 KJV).

In short, when God opens doors for you, it does not mean you will waltz through the doors with no challenges or opposition. Instead, it means you are to prepare for intense opposition, challenges, and obstacles. In fact, you ought to prepare for the fight of your life. Resistance is the hallmark of doing the will of God. It was not easy for Jesus as He surrendered His life for ours. Likewise, as a member of the body of Christ, it will not be easy for us to surrender our lives for the lives of others. Whatever God calls you to do in this life is not necessarily for your benefit but for the benefit of others. This conceptual blueprint for life will give you an understanding of the urgency of the matter concerning the world outside of you. One of my favorite kingdom sayings is "It is not about you." I am writing now under a self-imposed deadline simply because I hear the voice of God in my spirit saying, "Get it done. Get it done now!"

If you want to have a victorious life, you are going to have to fight for it. This is what it means to press. You have to go after it with all you have, and God will do the rest. Victorious life is not a life of perfection. It is a perpetual life of repentance and grace given to us by God. We will mess up sometimes, but never fail to get up from the mess! He uses us in spite of ourselves. So don't quit or give up! God has set us up for victory in Christ Jesus our Lord. God is not through with you yet. He has not given up on you. I do not pretend to know what God is saying to you or what He has called you to do concerning your purpose in life. I just know that whatever God has called us to do, He wants us to get it done!

God wants you to press past your self-imposed hindrances and excuses into His power so you can get it done! He wants us to experience the marvelous victory of His power. We must come into agreement with His will for our life. Next, we have to embrace and cooperate with that will of God, surrendering our past, present, and future to His will. Moreover, we must be willing to fight through hell and high water to see it come to pass. God has already given us the tools to get the victory! I will close this chapter with this influential and illustrative scripture found in the book of Ephesians, because it says it all. After you read this scripture, prepare to press into the power and get the victory!

> Now unto him that is able to do exceeding abundantly above all that we ask or think, according to the power that worketh in us, Unto Him be glory in the church by Christ Jesus throughout all ages, world without end. Amen. (Ephesians 3:20–21 KJV)

SECTION IV

THE SOURCE, THE SHIFT

CHAPTER 7

THE SOURCE

THE BIBLE AS THE SOURCE

This chapter will be one of the shortest chapters in the book, simply because it only contains the two passages of scripture that represent the core source of inspiration for this book. In my Christian journey, all inspiration comes from God. For me, there is no other true revelation on earth that does not originate from God. Some people ask me, "Does God still speak?" As I read His Word, He speaks loudly and clearly. He drops revelation daily. The more I read, the more I learn. I find new content and information in the Bible that I have been reading and learning since I was a child. The Bible is an ever-expanding text that grows with your varied experiences and level of maturity. Every time I read it, there is something in the text that causes me to develop a more in-depth understanding of God.

Hence, every time I read the Bible, I find something I must have missed or was not mature enough to understand in my previous interaction. As we grow spiritually and experience all that the world has to offer, it is important to synergize with God through His Word and the world to make sense out of our current reality. In other words, when I study the Bible, it brings clarity of thought and purpose to my life. As a result, it has a settling effect that causes me to calm down during uncertain times. Consequently, the Bible also helps me to understand the God in me, the world outside of me, and how I am to interact with both. The study of God's Word helps to shape my biblical worldview and my relationship with God. In my opinion, the reason so many people have a distrust or misinformation about God, church, and the Bible is purely due to a lack of biblical literacy. The Bible is probably the most talked about book that people have never read. This lack of understanding will automatically lead to a skewed perception of God and the church.

So, when I read Mark 2:1–12 (NKJV) and Luke 5:17–26 (NKJV), God began to give me insight like the sons and daughters of Issachar. I could see the sign of the times, and I understood what to do. The book was birthed out of an acute visual clarity, because I was literally 50 percent through another book that I started writing in October 2019. Then there was a shift, and the Lord literally spoke to my spirit and said, "Thank you for being faithful over that work. We will complete it, just not right now." So I shelved that book for an appointed period of time to be obedient to His voice in this season. My spiritual father taught me a long time ago that we cannot get caught up or stuck on what God said. We have to be very clear on what God is saying now in the present, or we will kill Isaac instead of the ram that God provided.

Mark 2:1–12 (NKJV) and Luke 5:17–26 (NKJV) represents the source of my inspiration for writing this book in God. If I was receiving a Word from God for a Sunday morning, this would be my focal pericope or the central focus of my message to the church. However, since this is a book and not a Sunday morning message, I will try to convey what God spoke to me with meticulous clarity. Equally important is your role as a reader. We have to begin with the same baseline for the impartation. So, in order for you to be blessed, take the time to read these two chapters. Read them several times if necessary. Slowly digest the content and let them sink in your spirit. Mark the passage with a pen or highlighter or both. Let God speak to your specific circumstance. The paralytic is likened unto the body of Christ, but he and his team are persistent. They refuse to give up on their quest to get into the presence of the Son of God. In times like these, with a whirlwind of problems and societal unrest, we all struggle to get into the presence of God, but if we fight hard enough, the reward will be greater than the struggle.

It's time to fight for the promises of God. It's time to embrace His resurrection power and to press to get into His presence. Now, I am not getting ready to give you a line-by-line or Sunday school expository lesson, so keep reading. These words of inspiration are still checking me and blessing me right up to this moment. The Word should check you so you can grow and develop in the things of God. We don't need a pacifier! We need the milk of God's Word to challenge us and move us out of our comfort zones and places of complacency. My prayer is simple: "God, move us like you moved the paralytic man and his team, in Jesus's name. Amen!" Remember to take your time and digest the Word of God. This Word will bless you if you let it marinate in your soul. God is speaking to you as you read the text. Open your heart to what He has to say!

THE SCRIPTURES

> And again He entered Capernaum after some days, and it was heard that He was in the house. Immediately many gathered together, so that there was no longer room to receive them, not even near the door. And He preached the word to them. Then they came to Him, bringing a paralytic who was carried by four men. And when they could not come near Him because of the crowd, they uncovered the roof where He was. So when they had broken through, they let down the bed on which the paralytic was lying. When Jesus saw

their faith, He said to the paralytic, "Son, your sins are forgiven you." And some of the scribes were sitting there and reasoning in their hearts, "Why does this Man speak blasphemies like this? Who can forgive sins but God alone?" But immediately, when Jesus perceived in His spirit that they reasoned thus within themselves, He said to them, "Why do you reason about these things in your hearts? Which is easier, to say to the paralytic, 'Your sins are forgiven you,' or to say, 'Arise, take up your bed and walk'? But that you may know that the Son of Man has power on earth to forgive sins"—He said to the paralytic, "I say to you, arise, take up your bed, and go to your house." Immediately he arose, took up the bed, and went out in the presence of them all, so that all were amazed and glorified God, saying, "We never saw anything like this!" (Mark 2:1–12 NKJV)

Now it happened on a certain day, as He was teaching, that there were Pharisees and teachers of the law sitting by, who had come out of every town of Galilee, Judea, and Jerusalem. And the power of the Lord was present to heal them. Then behold, men brought on a bed a man who was paralyzed, whom they sought to bring in and lay before Him. And when they could not find how they might bring him in, because of the crowd, they went up on the housetop and let him down with his bed through the tiling into the midst before Jesus. When He saw their faith, He said to him, "Man, your sins are forgiven you." And the scribes and the Pharisees began to reason, saying, "Who is this who speaks blasphemies? Who can forgive sins but God alone?" But when Jesus perceived their thoughts, He answered and said to them, "Why are you reasoning in your hearts? Which is easier, to say, 'Your sins are forgiven you,' or to say, 'Rise up and walk'? But that you may know that the Son of Man has power on earth to forgive sins" — He said to the man who was paralyzed, "I say to you, arise, take up your bed, and go to your house." Immediately he rose up before them, took up what he had been lying on, and departed to his own house, glorifying God. And they were all amazed, and they glorified God and were filled with fear, saying, "We have seen strange things today!" (Luke 5:17–26 NKJV)

THE WORD OF GOD IS OUR SOURCE

It would be impossible to think that a person could change their disposition without a catalyst, an igniter, or some type of external motivation. There will always be something or someone in your life that challenges you with a prescription for change. For me, the Word of God is that impetus for that change. In fact, I cannot press into the power of God without an accurate guidance system. That is what the Word of God represents to me. It is not just a book with a Judeo-Christian culture embedded in its text. It is a source of my life. The words on the pages of the Bible are not just inspirational; they are life, and these words provide me with wise counsel, practical wisdom for informed decision-making and learning the voice of God. The Word is a guide to learning how to press into the power. So, when I read the words from the text above, it is not just a literary narrative or a historical document. More importantly, it is a living testament, a life-giving treatise that demonstrates the power of God. The scripture is a blueprint for the potential impact available for my life and the lives of all people who will embrace its truth.

The words above speak to the harsh realities of life. Misfortune can overtake us in many different forms and cause us to miss portions of our life that others take for granted. As we go through life, we have many near-miss situations where we feel life is going to change, only to see a window of opportunity slip from our grasp. It is hard to embrace that it just was not our time or season. So we pluck along, developing a daily lifestyle that rallies around either the hope of endless expectation or the doldrums and stagnation of routine.

Not much is stated or known about the paralytic man and his support team. He seems to enter the Bible as an aside in Matthew 9:1–8 (NKJV). The focus is on the changing paradigm for priestly ministry as Jesus demonstrates to the religious leaders of His day what it means to be a priest after the order of Melchizedek. He is people oriented, and He is consistently moved by the actions of people who will go out of their way to prove that He has power to heal and restore. The paralytic is one such man who is somehow blessed to break out of the stagnation of excuses and despair. He finds or assembles a team of the right set of people who are determined to get him into the presence of God. They do not waver in their support of him, nor do they flinch in the sight of adversity. Whatever obstacles they have to overcome are transformed into opportunities to create pathways of success for getting into the presence of God.

So, when I read Mark 2:1–12 (NKJV) and Luke 5:17–26 (NKJV), I see a man with an obvious disadvantage taking a leap of faith on the word of either what he has heard or the nudging of God. When he takes this leap, he discovers the capacity of God to do something that has been beyond his control for years. He literally presses into the power of God with his team and is rewarded for his faithfulness. I believe God is still rewarding the faithfulness of His people, especially those who believe without seeing something in operation beforehand. Thus the scripture declares, "But without faith it is impossible to please Him: for He that cometh to God must believe that He is, and that He is a rewarder of them that diligently seek Him" (Hebrews 11:6 KJV). Remember, the Word of God is our source for radical change, and God will reward you if you learn to press into His power.

THE SOURCE AND CHANGING MINDSETS

When we receive Christ in our lives as our Lord and Savior and begin the process of reading the Word of God, there ought to be a radical shift in our thinking. If we indeed believe in the power of the Source and in the life-changing event that occurred on the day of our salvation, then there should be no doubt in our mind that God has the ability to change who we are and to present the seed for who we shall be in Him. In fact, we now have evidence that the God we serve can reach into our past and literally halt the progress of detriment and provide us with a cascade of grace. None of us deserve this favor, but our God is rich in grace and mercy. As a result, He blesses us in spite of ourselves. His plans for our lives are sovereign and cannot be altered because of the frailty and foolishness of humans. Instead, our proclivity to stray from His will is calculated into His plans for a direct divine outcome.

Furthermore and simply restated, God does not deal with humanity based on what we deserve. He deals with us based on the sovereign plans He has for all of humanity. His plans are independent of us. As I said earlier, they include us, but His plans cannot be influenced by us. He has calculated and included all possible outcomes. God cannot be surprised by our irrational behavior. He has built in contingencies for our proclivity to stray away from His original intent. He literally knows how to find us in a space of mutual cooperation, the space where we are ready to serve Him unequivocally.

At the point that His plan is ready to come to fruition, He will find us in whatever precarious place or position we have resolved to waddle in and take us through a process of divine restoration. We find His position incredulous because we all know that we are undeserving of this divine outcome, but His grace and mercy outweigh our negative and incapacitating thoughts about ourselves. In short, He will literally locate us wherever we are in life, and at the appointed time, He will locate us to fulfill our purpose. He found Moses on the backside of a desert, Joseph in prison, and Jesus in a borrowed tomb, and He will find you!

The story of Gideon is a prime example of how the GPS of God will find you and issue you your specific assignment for God's designated purpose for your life. Gideon was not in an ideal position. His people were being terrorized by the Midianites. There was no rest for the weary, and yet while he was threshing wheat in a wine press, God found him. When God has a plan for your life, He will find you too! Gideon was terrified because He was surrounded by the detriment of disobedience. Our negative decisions toward God on earth affect our present realities in a negative way. We reap what we sow. The past decisions of Israel to disobey God opened Pandora's box to the oppressive ways of the Midianites, who intimidated and terrorized Israel on a regular basis. However, He got a Word from the Lord that radically changed his view of life. Although Gideon had his doubts, he was ready to attack and destroy the idols of his father. He had to face his past in order to embrace his future.

He took on the customs and traditions of a city and found favor with God. God arrested his past and proved to him that His favor was brand-new. God was doing a new thing that was not necessarily like the favor that was on Gideon's ancestors. God was writing a new chapter in the history of Israel, and Gideon was chosen to be the main character. Look at this ironic tale. God will choose and use the person least qualified in the eyes of humans to bring radical change. How is that for irony?

Deliverance was in the hands of a man who fleeced God for a tangible response to a divine Word. When

God gives you a Word, there will be a radical shift in your mindset. It may start slowly and small like a fleeting thought or like a virus in a computer. Eventually, this fleeting thought will morph into a radical, life-changing experience that not only changes you but affects the body of Christ forever. Everyone who is connected to you and the people around you will be forever changed. Your light will shine in darkness, and the influence and impact of that light on your life will be noticed by all.

THE SOURCE AS A CATALYST OF CHANGE

The paralytic and his crew had to press into their future. They had to put up a fight in a hostile environment. Even now, we all have the potential to be changed because of their determination in the face of impossibility. As God was with them through adversity, so will He be with you! So, look at the potential outcome of pressing into your future. The future represents that which we have not seen. We access the future by faith. The future is filled with faith for the believer. Faith as defined in Hebrews 11:1 (KJV) as "the substance of things hoped for, the evidence of things not yet seen." Equally important is the fact that the future is also filled with favor. The favor of God is inexplicable because it represents the best of what God has to offer from an overflow of His well of love. It varies from person to person and can be described as the customized blessings of God being funneled through your life for the benefit of others. I believe God—that the best is yet to come. I believe your future is bright in Him. However, the road to the future must be paved by vehemently pressing through the bondages of your past circumstances and addictions.

Your mind has to break free of all the self-imposed barriers, the preexisting conditions, and cultural obstacles that are associated with your community. Self-imposed barriers are mindsets that are tethered to you because of your personal inadequacies or shortcomings. It is essentially how you view yourself or your self-worth. Preexisting conditions and cultural obstacles are challenges and stereotypes imposed or attached to the community in which you were born. In this setting, you have to live beyond the expectations of your village. You have to rise above the expectations of people. The Word of God is the source. It is your catalyst for radical change so you can overcome your limitations.

I have always heard people say, "Think outside of the box." I have never agreed with this statement in totality. However, I do understand the original intent. In my opinion, the box will always sit there as a constant reminder of the paradigm of constraint. A paradigm defined is a model or pattern. Thus, it is a model for what cannot be done. The box represents limitations and impossibilities. We must use the Word of God to get rid of the box. The paralytic and his crew literally removed the lid from their former customs and traditions to create another way of access to Jesus. Years ago, I modified the former statement to say, "Think as if there is no box." In that space, there is complete freedom in Christ. We are free to discover and explore who God created us to be and to achieve our ultimate purpose in Him.

Finally, once the Word becomes a true catalyst for radical change, we have to confront our present conditions. We have to look at our present situation and be determined to overcome them no matter what it takes. We have to press through our present situations, not using them as an excuse for inactivity or sedentary behavior. We cannot sit around and create barriers out of the negative things we can see in our daily environment. If we do, they will become stumbling blocks that can be used as an imposition or hindrance. In other words, any excuse will do. Do not let excuses block your progress. Your progress is like the light of a new day. Don't hinder what God wants to do with your current situation. Let the light of God shine in your life.

In your mind will always be the temptation to resist allowing God to alter the details of your current preexisting conditions and culture. Cut the cords of your past and the negative vacuum of your culture when necessary. My wife says it like this, "Don't let your past choke your future." Clear everything off the table of your present reality. Look past your reality and get a glimpse of your future. There is absolutely nothing in your present keeping you from your future but you. Get a clean slate and let God be God. Let this Word sink in your heart.

Don't just read the rest of this book for the sake of reading. Develop a habit of believing God against all odds. Let each word you read and each thought you capture motivate you to a brand-new existence in the kingdom of God. This is a season of radical change for the body of Christ. Everything starts with a renewed mindset in Christ. Let the Holy Spirit occupy its proper place on the throne of your heart. Submit to the will of God. Go on this divine journey and let God write a new narrative for your life. All things are possible to those who believe. The Source confirms this thought in the Gospel of Mark 9:23 (NKJV): Jesus said to him, "If you can believe, all things are possible to him who believes."

CHAPTER 8

THE SHIFT

THE DIVINE SHIFT

Out of the tragedy of the cross and the crucified Jesus came victory over the grave and death. The resurrected Christ had emerged! There was a shift in the theology and the understanding of God in the hearts of many who heard or experienced the resurrection. Suddenly there was the notion that what they knew about God was fractured and splintered, to say the least. Their faith was stirred to a new level. The preaching of Jesus and the cross caused a shift in the lives of thousands of people on the Day of Pentecost. The pneuma wind of God had come in the presence of the Holy Spirit, and nothing would ever be the same.

In the book of Exodus, the people of God were utterly bound and broken, but Israel eventually emerged with the spoils of their captives. It was the intervention of God in raising up a statesmen, a leader, named Moses. Moses was a man with a stick, a stutter, and an allegiance to God. Moses was a Hebrew raised in the palace and then exiled to the backside of the desert. It was his job to confront a stubborn and unyielding Pharaoh that caused a shift in the atmosphere. Finally, the authority of Pharaoh would be challenged by someone greater than himself. The plagues proved to be too much for Pharaoh, and he finally relented under the pressure of the God of Abraham, Isaac, and Jacob, even if it was only for a brief moment. It was all the time that was needed to free the people of God. The divine intervention of God turned a four-hundred-year cycle of captivity and oppression into a trip to the promised land.

The paralytic man represents the latent potential of the body of Christ in the story. He will experience a paradigmatic shift rising out of the sedentary ashes of despair to an active role in the vanguard of God. He was commissioned by God to go and tell his family. However, he was the most unlikely character to be given such a task after years of frustration. He was trapped in an immobile body, lying on a bed. How would a man without a suitable motivation convince four men to carry him around town? What would motivate him after years of watching life pass him by? Why would these men take time from their lives and personal goals to help him meet his goal of getting into the presence of God? What happened that made him vehemently press into the power of God? Perhaps he heard about the healing and miraculous power of God and said to himself, "If they can be healed, so can I." This decision would change his life forever. One word from the mouth of God can change your life forever. You can be crippled one day and walking the next.

This is called a paradigmatic shift, where out of evil or disparaging situations emerges good. It is inherent in our biblical understanding that all things work together for the good. Abraham's failed test with Pharaoh produced the grace of God and an increase in wealth. The horror of the lion's den produced an unscathed Daniel. This is the biblical motif of God producing blessings out of despair and the threat of imminent death.

In our text, God is once again doing a new thing. He uses the importunity or the perpetual determination of these five men to create a new dynamic for worship. They would not give up until they got in the presence of God! There were three unique shifts taking place in the text. These shifts represent the metanarrative or the big picture in scripture. It is the framework for the inner workings of the scriptures we will analyze in detail in section V. We will discuss three elements of the shift as outlined in detail below.

God was interrupting the normality of life and inserting a divine abnormality. A divine abnormality is what really should be happening on earth as a result of God's presence in the affairs of humans. God is ushering in a shift whenever He interrupts what we might consider to be normal. In short, before Jesus came on the scene, there should have been a plethora of healings and miracles with the proliferation of rabbis in ancient

Palestine. Instead, there was spiritual stagnation. Times like these are always ripe for a shift.

THE TRANSITION OF METHODOLOGY

When we read the text or the scripture, it shows us that the five men can no longer go through the front door because of the crowd, especially when one of them is on a bed and can't walk. Moreover, carrying a bed, they were not able to blend into the crowd within earshot of the voice of Jesus. In this season, we have to want more than just to blend in the crowd. God has not called us to blend into the crowd. He has called us to represent Him on earth.

God is persistent in His care for us. Everything about God is perpetual. So in the same manner that He looks after the sheep, we must seek Him. The five men were met with an impasse, but they found another way. We have to force the issue of getting in the presence of God. Our prayer life will have to become radical and raw. The darkness of our hearts has to be exposed to the light of God's presence, our negative habits checked and revealed. We have to fight to get into His presence regardless of the results.

The five men teach us that they had to change their methodology. In laymen's term, methodology is a way of doing things, a system for getting things done. All of us have methodologies whether we realize it or not. We have a system for cooking, brushing our teeth, driving, cutting the grass, investing, and reading the Bible. What can do more harm than good is continuing to use a methodology that is no longer functional or yielding fruit. The five men were willing to make a change.

Sometimes we need to change the way we do things. We need to change in order to create a more effective methodology. The five men were met with an impasse, and they decided to find another method for getting to Jesus. Yes, the method was unorthodox; however, it accomplished the goal of getting into the presence of God. The scripture teaches us that we need to get into the presence of God at any cost. In the times we currently live in, we have to be more flexible than ever before. We have to be able to shift with God. In this season, we need to put a demand on ourselves to get into the presence of God. Being in the crowd, spectating, is not going to cut it. We need to find a place in worship that yields the peaceable fruit of God.

If the front door is closed, we have to fight to create other access points to get in His presence. Sometimes we do not feel like praying or fighting. Sometimes our minds are so cluttered with the cares of this world, but we have to fight through whatever is holding us. Sometimes sin has sealed the access to the throne room, but we still have to fight with repentance and grace. Fight your personal demons. Fight to have a more intimate relationship with God. Fight to get past the flesh. Fight through marginal and basic prayer and get into His presence. Like the five men, if you fight, you will experience the power of God!

THE TRANSITION OF POWER

The text shows us that Jesus is surrounded by the religious leaders of the time. We could have identified these men by their postures, their haughty or proud looks, their phylacteries, or their flowing robes. They were known by their grand appearance. This appearance gave them the titles of priest, men of God, and yet they were unable to recognize the high priest in their midst. Today we can be actively involved in our churches and yet miss the move of God because we have buried our heads in the sands of religion. When we are preabsorbed in the ritual and predictability of church, we are irritated by a move of God that disrupts our normal flow, time schedule, and religious siesta. These men had become comfortable practicing the faith in their tombs of tradition. Everything was fine until John the Baptist showed up, crowds left the synagogues, and then out of nowhere comes this Jesus fellow. Clearly, the advent of Jesus represented a transition of power that would not be tolerated well by the powers that be at that time. Jesus was a problem to these men, so they followed him around, looking for a weakness they could exploit.

These men were members of the Sanhedrin. They were bound by the law and stuck in tradition. They were charged with taking care of the civil matters concerning the Jewish community under the rule of the Roman government. It was bad enough that they were subject to Roman authority. They were men in power without power. In other words, they were men who possessed the respect of their contemporaries because they had *exousia* power. This is the power of influence that comes along with a position or title. However, they did not have all power. Jesus had both exousia and *dunamis* power. Jesus had the power of influence that comes along with position and dunamis power or explosive power, the power to perform miracles and to do the impossible. That is the power to enforce His words or the will of the Father. It is the power to manifest and change things. Thus, when Jesus shows up on the scene, there is a shift in the balance of power. There was a transition that the Sanhedrin could not control, so they conspired to kill Him. (Confer with Matthew 12:9–14 NKJV; Matthew 26:3–4 NKJV; Matthew 27:1 NKJV; John 11:45–54 NKJV.)

The body of Christ in this generation is guilty of having exousia power with no dunamis power. We need to have a manifestation of God's Word in us to do simple things like being faithful to the call of God on our lives. Equally important is learning how to forgive and love unconditionally and resisting the bondages of sin. This takes dunamis power, especially to do it in a time when everyone is doing whatever they want to do, as if God is a deist who's aloof from us, while others act as if He is a God who does not exist or care about His creation. In fact, we tend to be all talk and some brief pockets of religious performance, but we have no true manifestation of the power of God on earth. Jesus, the true high priest, was in their midst with both powers in operation, and the men representing divine power did not recognize God in their midst. God was in the midst of us, right in the middle of a pandemic, and most people could not see His presence. This COVID-19 pandemic would have run crazy among us like the black plague or the Spanish flu—but for the sovereign hand of our mighty God! The five men in this story not only recognized God, but in the midst of an unfriendly and volatile environment, they risked all to be in the presence of the new sheriff in town. They were determined to experience the power of God!

THE EMERGENCE OF A NEW VANGUARD

As we close this chapter, we will explore the tenacity of the five men whose faith was admired by Jesus. Let's take a quick glance at the text as recalled by Luke in chapter 5:18–20 (NKJV): "Then behold, men brought on a bed a man who was paralyzed, whom they sought to bring in and lay before Him. And when they could not find how they might bring him in, because of the crowd, they went up on the housetop and let him down with his bed through the tiling into the midst before Jesus. When He saw their faith, He said to him, “Man, your sins are forgiven you.” There were men there all over and around the house, but most came to spectate. Some came to see what all the commotion was about in Capernaum. Others came to spy out the liberty of Christ and to see if what they said about Him was true. The Pharisees and the teachers of the law were there as self-serving members of the religious status quo, trying to preserve their own interest.

However, there in the mix of this quandary of men were four men who came to serve the interest of one paralytic by faith—a team of distinctive men, a new vanguard on a mission to see Jesus, because they believed He had power to heal. They were neither antagonistic nor curious, but they literally burst on the scene with a zeal and faith to get into the presence of the Son of the Living God. They were a new breed of men who had not been contaminated by the old. They obviously were not a part of the status quo, as represented by the reaction of the Pharisees and teachers of the law who pondered the credibility and the authority that Jesus had to forgive men of their sins. They were so intent on pressing into the presence of Jesus that they fabricated some kind of apparatus system for getting the paralytic off the ground and on top of the roof. This was a new vanguard of men who would not let any obstacles get in their way. They knew the urgency of their assignment, and they were rewarded with the manifestation of a miracle.

God was raising up men to effect change in their immediate community, which would ultimately spread beyond the expectations of people. Word of mouth was the chief vehicle for the spreading of news. There was no newspaper, phone, television, radio, or internet. News spread by virtue of one person telling another. Moreover, since Jesus did something amazing, He was the new talk of the town. Can you imagine? "Come see a man who can heal the lame." Men were astounded at the authority of Jesus telling the paralyzed man he was forgiven for his sins. They were utterly confused. The scribes were claiming that this act of forgiving sins belonged to God alone, and thus, Jesus was speaking blasphemies. They did not understand the power of God and the authority of His Son. They were especially taken aback by the immediate manifestation of the paralytic walking and being sent back to his family.

In spite of our current conditions, as members of the body of Christ, Jesus not only has the power to forgive but also the power to restore that which was dead, impossible, unimaginable, or unfathomable. What dead, impossible, unimaginable, or unfathomable situation are you currently going through? The body of Christ needs to know that God is still performing miracles. He is still able to do "exceedingly and abundantly above all we could ask or think according to the power that works in us" (Ephesians 3:20–21 NKJV). We need to press into the power of God in spite of what we see, think, or feel. We need to tear the roof off of our normal and make an open show of the enemy by getting into the presence of the Lord by any means necessary!

If you are willing to walk in obedience and do what God is calling you or has called you to do in this hour, regardless of the sacrifice, you are a part of this new vanguard. A vanguard is defined as a group of people who will blaze new paths and "lead the way with new developments or ideas" (*Oxford Dictionary*). They take the roof off of the status quo and represent "an advancing army" (*Oxford Dictionary*). These five men blazed a new path and represent an emerging vanguard. In the same way, God is calling for some of us to carry a similar mantle of responsibility. We are being called to blaze new paths and to defy that which has been considered normal. We are to fight to get into the power of God so we can hear His will clearly and be able to carry this will out with the absence of the fear of men and reprisal.

This will not be an easy task in this climate of anti-God sentiment. Walking out our salvation in fear and trembling is no longer a posture widely accepted by the masses. In other words, walking out our call with the proper respect and awe of God. We should fear no man, but we ought to revere God! You will be the minority in a sea of religion, dissenting philosophies, and moral relativism. Moral relativism basically asserts that everything is relative to what a person decides to believe. Essentially, whatever another individual believes is right about life and their standards for morality is correct. On the other hand, if you don't believe in morality, that is fine too. It is part of a greater move called postmodernism that refutes the validity of any moral standard for truth, especially the Bible. Part of the belief of postmodernism is that no one source or God is the standard or standard bearer for truth.

In fact, there is no absolute truth according to postmodernism. Truth is what you make it. This is going to be the deconstruction of societal norms as we have known it for the past century or longer. You will need an encounter with the presence of God to withstand the hurling accusations and insults that will come your way. This is a season where we will get a taste of the experience of what it might have been like to have lived during the time of Jesus. You will need a unique ear to discern the voice of God. Moreover, your eye must be focused on the eternal witness of the cross at Calvary. If you focus on the negativity that is in front of you, you will not be able to fulfill your assignment. Look up! Get to the roof! Tear the roof of your fears off and press into the amazing power of God!

One last thing you need to know is that the faith of the new vanguard is going to have to be radical. The reason Jesus was such a problem in His day was because everything about Him was radical. His prayer life was radical. He always went to a secret place to talk to His Father. Very rarely did He invite friends. The first time you hear Jesus inviting friends, they couldn't handle the intensity of His prayers, and they just fell asleep. His speech was radical. He was the tangible mouthpiece of God on earth. The dead and the sea obeyed His voice. His faith was radical. He did not believe there was anything impossible for Him to do through the Father, including laying down His life for the brethren and being resurrected on the third day. Jesus was incredibly radical, preaching and teaching on the side of mountains or on lakes while standing in a fisherman's boat. He hung out with people who would be considered the dregs of society. For all intents and purposes, if He was alive in the flesh today, He would be considered off the chain.

In closing, these five men had radical faith. When you get to the roof, you have to press into what you can no longer see. Jesus could have moved, left, or refused to see them, but they pressed in by faith nevertheless. They dismantled the roof and released the paralytic right into the presence of the power of God! Jesus was awed by the radical faith of these men. He forgave the paralytic of sin. Jesus then used him as an object lesson for the emergence of a new vanguard. In spite of the negative interjections and dispositions of the Pharisees and teachers of the law, Jesus still moved in the power of God. Jesus told him to take up his mat and go to his house. Radical faith yields radical results! The power of God transcends hostile environments and the opinions of people. God is indeed sovereign!

SECTION V

AUTHORITY, BONDAGE, AND HOPE

CHAPTER 9

AUTHORITY AND CONDITIONS

AUTHORITY TO FORGIVE

Forgiveness is a critical theme in this text. There is something that is uncommon about the presence of Jesus. When we understand who He is and what He represents, it can change our lives. Many people have come into the presence of Jesus, including demons, and immediately recognized His deity and His authority on earth (Matthew 8:29 NKJV; Mark 1:24 NKJV; James 2:19 NKJV). If demons acknowledge the authority of the Son of God, could it be that the paralytic and his team also knew? They went to extraordinary lengths to press into His power. Did they possess internal intel? Was it a gut feeling? Maybe it was divine inspiration or word of mouth that led them to believe that Jesus had power. Their understanding was critically important, especially since most people thought He was just an itinerant preacher with uncommon gifts or a community rabble-rouser, as suspected by many of His religious contemporaries.

What happens when we really believe in the power of God to transform? I believe it stripped the paralytic of every sense of pride and exposed his guilt and nakedness before the Lord. In other words, when we come before the presence of the Lord, we must believe like the Hebrew writer in chapter 11:6 (NKJV), "that He is and that He is a rewarder of those who diligently seek Him." In fact, like Adam and Eve, we must be willing to come before Him "naked and ashamed" and yet know that His love will cover the multitude of our sins and faults. Remember, we have an advocate with the Father in Jesus the Christ. God wants to heal us of our sins more than He wants to heal our natural bodies. Why? Simply because the natural body shall pass away. It is our spirit self that shall remain and inherit the things of God. Thus, it is critically important that our souls are right with God.

Moreover, it is clear why Jesus forgave his sins before He told him to walk. Now, imagine being the paralytic, embarrassed and feeling unworthy because of his past transgressions, being lowered before Jesus in the midst of a group of strangers. However, God honors the efforts and the persistence of people, and in the midst of being exposed before the people, he is overtaken by the presence and power of the Son of God. When you truly get in the presence of God, everything around you will become unimportant. All fear and negative thoughts and the visage of negative people dissipate under the power of His presence. It is as if you have been translated temporarily to a different place. Time stops, and you recognize that God is real and that this experience is not a figment of your imagination.

Hence, Jesus, knowing all about his past and the former exploits of the paralytic, blesses him and bares the burdens of his sins like he is an errant child. Jesus has mercy on him and immediately forgives his sins. In His authority, Jesus knows the thoughts and intents of our hearts. He can see our sins a mile away. He spares this man the guilt and shame of feeling unworthy in His presence and forgives his sins. Either way, whether the paralytic came to expose his sins or Jesus relieved him of the burden of sin because of a contrite heart and a broken spirit, Jesus has the authority to forgive.

Unrepented sin can be a spiritual weight. It can cause us to live beneath the privilege and power inherent to those of us who name the name of Christ. There will come times in our lives where we are so broken in the presence of God He will raise up and expose layers of unrepented sin—things we have forgotten about or past sins of omission that we did not commit intentionally, but we got caught up in our own delusions. God raised Jesus from the dead to give Him all authority and power in the heavens and the earth. Why live our whole lives as believers and never press into His power? A part of our transformation in Christ during this season is not only recognizing who He is but recognizing that He has power that He exclusively wants to share with us. We don't have to lie on our beds forever. Like the paralytic man, we must recognize that we have a Savior who wants to forgive us and give us the power to walk again.

On the other hand, the scribes and the Pharisees were spiritually ignorant and naturally arrogant. They were in disbelief that Jesus could forgive sins. In fact, from their perch, only God could forgive sins! Look at their blindness. They were sitting in front of God, Jesus the Christ, God's representative and Son on earth, and because He was not in their circle of associates, they were blinded. They were more interested in His potential to empty their synagogues and shift the balance of power, rather than being concerned about healing people and being obedient to what God was saying and doing in their presence.

The pandemic and its aftermath will give us periods and points of reflection. As we both reflect and press closer into the presence of God, there should be a level of conviction that surfaces. Do not trade this moment or opportunity consumed in social media or hanging your head in despair. There is hope and healing for the body of Christ. The promises of God are still obtainable. It is not over yet. Remember, the enemy wants us to think our time has passed. The devil is a liar.

Let me reiterate that when we really press into His

presence with sincerity of heart, things that were forgotten will make their way to the front of our consciousness. God will begin to purge our hearts of things we may have never repented of, or He will remind us about people we never forgave. He will give you the power to forgive and to be forgiven. Only those of us with clean hands and a pure heart can approach His holy mountain. Herein lies His throne of grace. We have to desire His presence more than His presents. His presence will reveal His plans for our lives and give us access to His power.

Pressing into the plans and purposes of God for our lives calls for a clean heart. Notice, before Jesus gave the paralytic power to walk, He first forgave his sins. If we want the pure presence of God in our hearts, we have to be willing to clear our hearts of the clutter of baggage. This baggage will keep God from filling our hearts with the complete power of His presence. Stepping up to be in God's vanguard will require a clean and pure heart—a heart that forgives and a heart that recognizes the need to be forgiven.

NATURAL CONDITIONS IN A NATURAL REALM

God is saying that the church suffers from a myriad of issues that must be remedied in order to be effective in this next season of ministry. Listed below are some of the natural conditions that hinder the modern church.

We need to shake these things off of us like a snake into the fire at Malta. We must learn to trust God and to no longer be bound by our mind's inability to embrace the power of God. Open your heart today and get ready to press into the power of God! In Jesus's name, we will never think ourselves out of God's will ever again!

1. *The paralysis of analysis.* The paralysis of analysis is overthinking everything, so much so that we overthink ourselves out of the plans of God for our lives. The body of Christ is literally stuck in time in the natural realm. We are waiting around for a good time or a time without trouble to do what God said. Simultaneously, we are losing precious time trying to determine God's will and to understand His plans for our lives. For some insane reason, we feel the need to help God out. We are not moving forward or backward. We are just stuck in a revolving time warp, waiting for everything to line up for what we perceive as success, which can only emerge at the right time, which never comes. The fact of the matter is that God's success is just the opposite. When all odds are stacked against us is when God does his best work.
2. *Catatonic stupor.* It is a state or syndrome of not being able to move. Take, for example, the battle between the orca, king of the sea on top of the

apex predator food chain, and the dethroned former apex predator, the great white shark. The orca or killer whale is the supreme hunter. It is smarter, larger, and faster than the great white. In fact, it knows how to attack the great white shark in such a way that knocks the shark on its back and renders it helpless. When you flip certain species of sharks upside down on their back, the shark can no longer swim or move. It becomes immobile and is in a type of catatonic stupor better known as tonic immobility. When trials, tribulations, pandemics, or the attacks of the enemy hit the body of Christ, most of the time it puts us in a catatonic stupor. We must learn to overcome this state of immobility. We must learn to call on the name of Jesus to free us from this state of indecision and stagnation. We must decide that we want to live again. The power to live and to walk again are in the presence of the Lord!

3. *Stuck between the valley of disappointment and the peak of panic.* Life or somebody has disappointed you. You almost feel like everything in life is set on keeping you from completing the assignments of God. People you trusted and loved hurt you; a promotion fell through; a failed relationship; some kind of church hurt or some mountain slide of negative events has tried to derail or impede

> your progress. God is calling us to rise out of this valley of disappointment. Every disappointment is "working for us a far more and exceeding and eternal weight of glory" (2 Corinthians 4:17 NKJV). Embrace your disappointment and move on. All things, including this negative period of time, are working together for your good.

As we transverse the mountain of life, we have the peak of the mountaintop in view. However, for some reason, we are afraid to finish the climb, maybe because the number of people we started with has diminished and we wanted everyone to be blessed. You have to remember God gave you the assignment. The assignment was yours alone to complete. You will help more people by finishing the course. Continue mapping the route to the top through prayer, determination, and total commitment to achieving the plans of God for your life. Don't look back.

Remember this: the air is thinner at the top of the mountain. It may feel like you can't breathe until you make the mental and anatomical adjustments. In the same way, when we begin to walk in God's will for our lives, we will have unique experiences. You will have to make some spiritual adjustments. In time, you will become comfortable walking in this trail of blessings and encountering intense warfare with the enemy along the way. Continue to trust God every step of the way.

On the other hand, many of us are afraid of the elevation, or we have a fear of the unknown and uncertainty, but we have to press into the places where God wants us to be. We can't panic and abort the mission before it is complete. Furthermore, sometimes we make it to the peak of panic, and because of the cloud cover, we can't see the victory that lies in the valley below. Just remember, you may have come out of the valley of the shadow of death on one side; however, that does not mean that the valley on the other side of the mountain is going to be full of dry bones. In fact, the valley on the other side is a valley of greater growth and fertility. In this season, your latter will be greater than your former. Prepare to experience the Valley of Berachah (2 Chronicles 20:25–28).

4. *In survival mode rather than success and operation mode.* Many people in the body of Christ are in survival mode. They are just trying to get by and make it, as if they serve the God of just a little or barely enough. The fact of the matter is that we serve the God of exceeding abundance who has given us everything that pertains to life and godliness (2 Peter1:3). Moreover, the book of Genesis affirms that we were created in His image and given *dominion* (power and authority in the earth realm) to reign on earth. We have been given power to be *fruitful* (productivity), to *multiply*

(reproduction/discipleship), to *replenish* (power to give back and to help others), and to *subdue* (to govern, rule, control). If we are not walking in this or at least toward this, we are living beneath our privilege. As stated earlier, time is the most valuable commodity in the world. God has given us the privilege of time redemption, and we need to make haste in "redeeming the time for the days are evil" (Ephesians 5:16 KJV). Do it now! Once you capture the essence of time redemption, there needs to be a sense of urgency that overruns the spirit of fear and complacency to meet God on this platform of expectancy. We have not been called to live a life of despair; we have been given the victory by God through our life in the Lord Jesus Christ! This is not the end of your rope. Let go of your rope and fall into the abundance of God.

5. *Afraid of the demons at the door.* When we examine 1 Corinthians 16:9, we will discover that as God opens these great and effectual doors in our lives that no man can shut, there will be adversaries, haters, enemies, demons, or mushrooming opposition standing in the doorway. However, "no weapon formed against you shall succeed" (Isaiah 54:17 CSB). We have to take courage and stand bold in the midst of demonic opposition. Like Joshua and Nehemiah, we have to confront

> the enemy and take on our fears face-to-face. We cannot live a life afraid of demons or people being used by them. Demons are subject to the will of God. Thus, when they are unleashed in our lives, it is only a test. We have to pass the test! We have to overcome with the blood of the lamb and the words of our testimonies. Each conquered test will give us new and fresh testimonies.

We must master the art of conquering the enemy, just like Jesus did in the wilderness against Satan. He confronted Satan with the Word of God and got the victory. We cannot avoid the adversaries in the door. They have been put there to help us gain spiritual confidence. Similarly, in the garden, in a crucial conversation with His Father, Jesus revealed His humanity. Take this cup from me Lord; nevertheless not my will but thine will be done (Matthew 26:42 KJV). Therefore, take courage! It is normal then to feel like we cannot achieve the will of God for our lives. However, we also cannot stand at the door of destiny and opportunity and cower. Instead, we must proclaim the goodness of the Lord in the land of the living and march forward with the full armor of God, having the confidence and knowing that God will prevail! Just remember, it is never too late. That door of opportunity is still open to you today (Revelation 3:8 NLT)!

CHAPTER 10

HOPE IN THE MIDST OF DETRIMENT

HOPE FOR OUR SPIRITUAL DISPOSITIONS

Trouble, like a pandemic, socioeconomic uncertainty, and political unrest, will always reveal the stress points and fractures in the armor of those of us who represent the body of Christ. Listed below are some of the obvious places of vulnerability that oftentimes hinder the progress of the body. Each section provides a model of shifting change. God will move if we are ready to move with Him. Thus, in order to press into the power of God, we have to take ownership of our blind spots and shortcomings. We have to face them head-on with prayer and the fierce determination of an advancing army. In short, we have to take consistent responsibility for our actions while fighting to follow the mandates of God's Word.

Note, this will not be an easy fight. However, you will win in Christ if you possess pit bull–like faith. Once you discover the will of God for your life, don't let go!

No matter what may arise. Fight to press into His power! Fight to come into agreement with God's will for your life. It is at this point that God's power will be released. Heaven has equity in the will of God and hence will always release the power of God when we cooperate with God's will for our lives.

Christianity has often been misunderstood and mischaracterized. In many circles, it is a religious experience characterized by a lifetime of sheltered service in the church. This secularized approach to Christianity limits its scope and influence. Christianity in its original intent was always designed to both impact and influence the world around it. Moreover, the core of the Christian faith was the embodiment of a lifestyle of worship to God. Our lives should be representative of who God is on earth. Our endeavor and aim should be to please Him. Case in point, our daily practices should be intertwined with the core tenets of our faith. Life is intertwined in the faith, and true Christian faith is the essence of life. Thus, in the faith, we are either fighting our way out of something or fighting our way through something, but we are always in some kind of fight. The five points below represent some of the struggles inherent to pressing into the power of God!

1. *We are stuck between the porch and the altar (Joel 2:17 NKJV).* The book of Joel calls for the priest to weep between the porch and the altar. This

> was an act of contrition or repentance needed for the people of that day in order to be restored to the will of God. With each passing generation, we tend to move further and further away from God. Thus, today, our need is greater because our generation has lost their way. As a result, many of us who should be leading the way have surrendered ourselves to a place of complacency, compromise, and corruption. By corruption, I mean we have a virus that has subtly invaded our spirits and caused us to stray from the timeless foundations of our faith.

Many Christians no longer see the need to read and study the Word of God. People can take or leave church, and when they do come, there is a lack of coherence between the listener and the sender. The senders think they are being ignored. The listeners, on the other hand, feel a need to critique every other word, using what my wife calls the "Google god." Hence, we are stuck between the porch and the altar, not weeping but in contemplation. We are questioning the validity and integrity of the faith from the pulpit to the pews. We are locked in a state of limbo or indecision that has slowed the progress of the body. We need a word from the Lord!

We are trying to choose between embracing the porch, which represents the flesh, and the altar, which represents the Spirit. Moreover, the altar also represents an enduring relationship with the Lord. We are in a crisis of decision. God is calling his church to true repentance. The church needs to respond by asking forgiveness of our sins but also by being willing to turn from our sins. We all need to run to the place of intimacy in this season. We need to abandon limbo and run back to the altar of our God. We need God more than anything in the earth right now! We need to embrace learning how to live for God while we allow Him to live through us! It's time to put our lives on the altars of mercy and grace.

As a matter of consequence, it is high time for us to completely surrender our minds, hearts, bodies, and souls to the will of God, continuing in the process of regeneration in Christ. In other words, we need to continue in the process of growing in our salvation. Many believers quit Christianity because of something they heard or saw in the church long before they were toddlers in the faith. They are sheep without the concern and love of a shepherd. Like a mother calls her children, at the end of the day, God is calling His elect home. Paul said it best in Romans 12:1–2 (KJV), "I beseech you therefore, brethren, by the mercies of God, that ye present your bodies a living sacrifice, holy, acceptable unto God, which is your reasonable service. And be not conformed to this world: but be ye transformed by the renewing of your mind, that ye may prove what is that good, and acceptable, and perfect, will of God." Eugene

H. Peterson's Message Bible puts a contemporary spin on this timeless word:

> So here's what I want you to do, God helping you: Take your everyday, ordinary life—your sleeping, eating, going-to-work, and walking-around life—and place it before God as an offering. Embracing what God does for you is the best thing you can do for him. Don't become so well-adjusted to your culture that you fit into it without even thinking. Instead, fix your attention on God. You'll be changed from the inside out. Readily recognize what he wants from you, and quickly respond to it. Unlike the culture around you, always dragging you down to its level of immaturity, God brings the best out of you, develops well-formed maturity in you. (Romans 12:1–2)

2. *The pool of Bethesda (John 5:1–9 NKJV).* The church must understand that this season cannot be controlled by the flesh. Moreover, this is not a time of normality. There is nothing mundane or usual about this time. The way things used to happen to us, or our normal modus operandi, is getting ready to be disrupted by the supernatural will of God. There is going to be an invasion

> of epic proportions of both time and space. In other words, things that would take us years to accomplish will happen in a very short period of time. Similarly, things that we have had to endure for extended periods of time are about to change suddenly. Those of us who are lining up to cooperate with the will of God for our lives are going to experience a shift. This sudden shift will be so divine that only God, exclusively, will be able to get the glory!

The paralyzed man in this text has to change his mindset, which will alter the position of his heart. He can no longer lie or sit at the pool with the impotent, hopeless, pessimistic, and powerless people who trust in the arm of the flesh. Our trust must rather be in the hand of God. Their trust had been blinded by the lapse of time and the sedentary state of their lives. In the same way, today we cannot sit in the pews or chairs week after week with no expectations. There is a testimony with your name written on it. Consequently, you have to have a desire to rise to the occasion. The normal way of waiting haplessly for an angel or someone to do something for you is being disrupted. God has a plan. Today is a new season. God is coming for His people. God interrupted the dismal life of the paralytic at the pool and gave him an unexpected infusion of hope and victory. Whatever we are going to do in Him will be punctuated when we willingly say yes and rise at His command.

We have to embrace change, letting go of the former to embrace the latter, forgetting the failures of the past and walking into the blessings of our now. The promise is here! Pick up your mat. Your mat represents all of your issues and problems. All of your disappointments will not disappear at one time. However, you will get the opportunity to introduce the disappointments of your past to the promises of your future. By faith, you have to walk with God into your promise. Herein lies the change in mindset. The fulfillment of the promises of God for our lives were never based on our perfection but on His perfection. He alone is sufficient in our time of weakness (2 Corinthians 12:9 KJV).

3. *Sitting outside of the gates of Samaria (2 Kings 7:1–12 NKJV).* The church must be willing to move in times of desperation. We must be willing to trust God when we have no idea where He is in our lives. Our concept of God must expand beyond our emotions and senses. We must boldly trust Him according to His tried and unfailing Word. There comes a point in time spiritually where we know that He is and that He will honor His promises and plans toward us no matter what, especially in the night hour when we cannot see outcomes. We cannot sit around waiting for perfect conditions.

> Perfect conditions will never come. In fact, God does not get the glory in perfect conditions. However, when conditions are dire, the hearts of the people are failing, the government is faltering, and a nation is teetering on the brink of disaster, that is when God will get the glory. It is in these critical moments when God shines and does His best work. He operates best when we are at our worst in impossible conditions.

Furthermore, when we are in the times that seem hopeless, when all has seemingly failed, that is the time we need to move in God. God has already gone before us in anticipation of our next move. Like a world-class chess player, God has already outwitted and outmaneuvered the enemy. The enemy in the gates and the fields has already been crippled and defeated by the power of our God. The weapons and devices of the enemy have backfired on him. Move swiftly, saints! The same army of chariots and horses sent by God that surrounded the Syrian army threatening Elisha and his servant is the same divine army that caused the Syrians to flee in this text, leaving food and supplies to bail out an entire city in despair. This same army has been loosed in this season on our behalf.

The four leprous men had a choice to stay still and die or to walk into the unknown. They chose to live and decided to travel the road of uncertainty and potential death. However, God prevailed in the place of potential death, and it became the place of life and abundance. Everything around us is crazy now—the pandemic, death, unemployment, pain, suffering, greed, anarchy, social and political unrest. God is telling us to move in this time of desperation and confusion. A way of escape has already been prepared. Lord, open our eyes that we may see that you have our backs and have made a way out of no way in this season!

4. *Tripping on the seas of adversity when Jesus is in the boat (Mark 4:35–41 NKJV).* Stop tripping! God is with us! The times we live in are not a surprise to God. These are indeed adverse and perilous times, but like the paralytic and his team, we must see God moving in the midst of the storm. God is sovereign, and we have been selected to go through this windstorm. It seems like God is asleep, but He is fully aware of what is going on with us. He has given us His Son to help us manage the storm. We must draw strength from His ability to rest in God through the storm. He is asleep on the stern, or what we call the back of the boat, but He is not dead. He is fully aware of the times we are living in and the treacherous situations we will encounter. Jesus has our backs, and He will arise from the stern of our lives at the appointed time!

God has not called us to trip, losing our minds because we are focused on the impending doom. In our humanity, we often create fret over the potential of our demise in this season. This is a live training ground. At all times, we must be alert and prepared for the wiles or tricks of the devil. Mark this in your spirit: we will survive the storm simply because we belong to Him and the devil is no match for our God. Secondly, He is the Master of the storm, and the storm obeys the voice of God. Just as the pandemic came out of nowhere, it will cease at the command of our God. "Peace. Be still!" We must learn to rest in adversity. When we rest, it is a sign that we know our God and that we know what He is capable of doing when the appropriate time comes. Jesus will wake Himself if and when it is necessary. In order to press into His power, you must first believe that He has power.

5. *Hiding in the house, and Jesus appears (John 20:19–23 NKJV).* It was one of the most chaotic and precarious times in the history of the early church. Jesus was supposedly dead, and the disciples were securely locked in their home, threatened by the possibility of a certain death. If you think about it, this circumstance was not just unique to this time in history. Today, our situations are very similar. The body of Christ is locked in their homes with the rest of the world, because we too

> fear for our safety. In this modern era, most people were living in fear of COVID-19 or the Omicron variant. On the other hand, the disciples were afraid of the Jews. Jesus obviously came through doors that were locked and stood in their midst. What a time to release a praise! Death, the grave, the stone, and all the other inanimate objects, like the doors or walls of the disciples' homes, could not stop the progress and power of our God through Jesus Christ our Lord.

Jesus came and stood right in the midst of their fear to prove that He could not be disregarded or minimized. Jesus was alive! The resurrection was real! Jesus had risen from the dead as promised in the scripture, and He was standing among the disciples in person. His life and position took on new meaning as the resurrected Savior. They saw him down and out, broken, battered, bruised, unrecognizable, and to the point of death. Now here He was, the Son of the Living God, a vision of health, healing, resurrection power, and the glory of God!

In the midst of fear and turmoil, Jesus brings peace. As He showed His hands and side, He also released them to walk in His power by breathing on them, saying, "Receive the Holy Spirit," and then He taught them forgiveness of sins. The power of God was released in them through the Holy Spirit and the knowledge of forgiveness. We need to ask God to forgive us and to allow the power of God to move through us in this season. The body of Christ needs to exchange the mindset of fear for the power of God's Word! Whatever He told you to do, do it! Press into His power! It is time for us to stop being afraid to walk in our destiny!

CHAPTER 11

THE PRESS AND THE BED

THE DECISION TO PRESS

God is calling the church to press into Him for forgiveness of sins. This pressing in or fighting past all hindering obstacles will release spiritual healing and power. We need forgiveness of our sins to be able to carry out our assignments, with the freedom and power that flows with ease, through those who have clean hands and a pure heart. We need power to endure the attacks of the enemy and to persevere through time and situations that cause us to want to quit before the promise. We need power to walk out our salvation, to grow in grace, and to fulfill our purpose in Christ. Taking a close look at Luke 5:17 (NKJV), it states, "And the power of the Lord was present to heal Him." We often seek the face of God for presents and things; however, in this dispensation, we need the healing and forgiving hand of God. We need His healing powers working in us and through us, or we will not survive. We have to be the joints that supply one another's needs (Ephesians 4:16 KJV).

The enemy attacks our minds daily because it's the foci of decision-making! He uses "the twin towers" to work our minds over. He knows that it is very difficult to make good decisions when we are frustrated. The twin towers of disappointment and discouragement are like a one-two punch to the gut. Disappointment always opens the door for discouragement, and we have to guard against these foes that attack the mind intermittently. Symbolically, our minds are being saturated with the flesh associated with the porch that was outside of the Holy Place. The porch in the days of the Temple of Solomon was the place and steps that led to the Holy Place. If the doors were open and you stood on the porch, the Altar of Incense representing the prayers of the saints would be in front of you. From the same position, the Altar of Sacrifice would be behind you to the right, representing the place where the flesh of animals were sacrificed for the remission of sins. The porch then can take on the symbolic posture of being the place of decision. Either I go into the Holy Place and inhale the sweet and savory fragrance of His presence or I stay out on the porch and inhale the putrid smell of burning animal flesh. Similarly, God allows us to make that choice daily. We have to choose between the things that please the flesh and the things that please God.

Pressing will always require a decision to be made

between the flesh and the Spirit. If you are going to press into the presence of God, you cannot have both. You have to make up your mind. We are constantly being bombarded by the media and social media platforms, which have become like a surrogate church consuming inordinate amounts of time and brain capital. The enemy is trying to make us think that we will be paralyzed in our current situations and predicaments forever. He has tricked the saints into believing that nothing will ever change. So we need forgiveness to free our minds of our sinful thoughts, habits, and inhibitions. Forgiveness will loose or release the healing power of God.

We are going to have to develop some new spiritual habits. Like the paralytic, we are going to have to press past the crowd. Our past is in the crowd. Our "friends" are in the crowd. Delay and disappointment are in the crowd. Betrayal and failures are in the crowd. Time is in the crowd, screaming, "It's too late!" Doubt is in the crowd, yelling, "Don't even think about it!" Haters are in the crowd. Negative thoughts are in the crowd, along with doom and gloom. Religion is in the crowd. Yes, we have been approaching God the same way, praying the same prayers and expecting different results. That repetition that used to be a fresh anointing is now stale, and it reeks of religion. The enemies of our destiny and purpose are in the crowd, and for the first time, we must rise above them. I have outlined a couple of steps that will assist you in pressing into His power.

First, we are going to need to learn how to be persistent and unyielding. To press has the connotation of pushing in until something happens or a desired outcome is released. Being tenacious and importunate should be synonymous with our character when our names are uttered in the spirit realm. In other words, we should be known in the spirit realm for having pit bull–like tendencies. We won't let go until you bless me. We will keep asking, seeking, and knocking even to the point of potential annoyance. If the front door is blocked, we will find another access point.

Secondly, we must comprehend that initially people won't be able to help us. This is going to start between you and the Holy Spirit. The paralytic had to have made his mind up long before his help showed up. You will be alone and misunderstood for a season. However, do not languish in discouragement. We have a guarantee that the Spirit shall prevail. He will engulf you like a lava in a cocoon until a new you emerges. When you emerge from this place of transformation, you will have obtained a level of spiritual maturity that allows you to pursue your purpose. Don't be afraid to be alone for a season. If you study the Word carefully, most of the characters that God used in the Bible suffered through a season of obscurity, but obscurity will give way to the purposes, destiny, and glory of God. Just hold on!

WHO'S CARRYING YOUR BED?

The bed that must be carried represents your purpose, problems, promise, and vision. Often times, people think that when you are in pursuit of the will of God that all of your problems and situations must be in order. Quite the contrary, you will have to work on solutions to these situations and problems, while simultaneously pursuing the will of God. In fact, some of your most polemical problems will fall away as you pursue God's will for your life. That is why it is a press—because this can be one of the most difficult periods of your life. Moreover, as a backdrop, you will still be dealing with the issues of your past that try to tether themselves to your future. In short, you have to learn to walk away from your past. The time you have spent there will make it difficult, but it can be done. Remember, your past will never embrace your future. However, once you start on this path to embracing your future, you have to put one foot in front of the other and not look back. Hence, walk out of your past into your future.

This will entail developing some new relationships. You may already know these people from another season of your life, but now is the time for your relationship to grow. The people you have overlooked in your past are ready to help you transition into a new way of living. Remember, you will have to be surrounded by the right kind of people—people who have uniquely been sent to you by God for the expressed purpose of getting you past this gauntlet of dynamics and into your future. These new companions will help you execute the will of God in your life. Who is going to help carry your bed? These four men were determined to get the paralytic into the presence of God in spite of extremely hostile conditions.

Since there is nothing new under the sun, it would hold true that human nature was the same then as it is today. Thus, the paralytic and his team had to endure insensitive insults and harassments to complete their assignment, people saying things like, "Go home!" "There is no more room." "Try another time." "You are in the way. Move it!" "Get down from there!" "You are wasting your time. Jesus doesn't want to see you!" "Get your crazy self out of here!" However, these men would not leave until the mission of getting into the presence of God was fulfilled. The paralytic had hooked up with some genuine brothers who were willing to carry the paralytic and his vision to great heights to see the promises of God fulfilled over his life. Who's helping you? Can they see past your problems to the promise? Who is carrying your bed?

In this current season, we are experiencing great change. We are in the midst of a shift, and we must learn to shift as well. Thus, the church or the body of Christ is required to examine relationships in a shift. We should start with our relationship with God. Are you on fire or just barely getting by? Are you being suffocated by the smoke of religious practices? Make the shift now. Next, we must examine all of our friends and other relationships. You can't worship with everybody, and you can't pursue purpose with everybody. Sometimes you have to go all in when you worship, bypassing the crowd and your usual entrance into the presence of God and creating another point of access. The way you used to worship God won't ever work for you again!

This means going higher in the faith, higher in worship—like the paralytic and his team, removing all barriers and obstacles to get into the presence of God. There are critical moments where the roof has to be removed from our worship. We have to break in and break through to get into the presence of our God! Samuel R. Chan wrote a leadership book called *Who's Holding Your Ladder?* It talks about the dynamics of your supporting cast. My question to you is, Who is helping to carry the vision that God gave you? Just remember that Uzziah died, Judas betrayed, and Barnabas left Paul because of John Mark. However, Caleb, Hannah, and John the beloved were faithful to the end.

EXAMINE YOUR ACQUAINTANCES

Many of you are surrounded by too many toxic and unhealthy relationships. Streamline and test your relationships. The crutch syndrome says you need these people when you actually don't. Walk away from these false relationships. Lean on Jesus and press into His power.

1. *Fake friends* are surrounding you, but it is for their own self-aggrandizement or what we would call false pretenses and personal gain. They hang with you because there are benefits that they derive from being around you. They are takers and add nothing to your life.
2. *Dream killers* never support your dreams or vision. They carry semiautomatic silencers (their tongues). When you are blessed or something good happens to you, they don't say much. They offer no real or genuine support. In fact, most of them don't say anything at all. They go into silent mode or change the subject. Deflection is how they hide their envy. They secretly desire what you have. Others use the power of their tongues to kill your dreams with a barrage of negativity.
3. *Frenemies* are very dangerous. They are people in your life who seriously want to kill you and your spirit. They can disguise their jealousy for years. They have something that they fear you will take from them. They try to keep you down. They use their tongues to spew poison and disguise it in humor; however, they mean exactly what they say. Their words are both harmful and injurious.

Do not underestimate the power of the tongue to create an atmosphere of death and life when spoken over your life. This person wears a demonic mask of deception. They usually get very close to you, but they will turn on you when you least expect it or when you need them the most. Remember this: put your trust in no man.

4. *Haters* will assume the pseudo posture of being friends. They will do just enough to hang around, but in all actuality, they hate you. These people often dislike you for no reason at all. They have a dual purpose for keeping you around. First, they always want to know what you are doing, but they never want to tell you what they are doing. Your life intrigues them, and they keep you close so they can secretly imitate and mirror your style, charisma, personality, potential, or position.

Secondly, they secretly hope for your demise or failure. They secretly derive great pleasure or joy from watching bad things, negative events, and unfortunate occurrences in your life. They are both jealous and envious of you—jealous because they don't want you to have what they possess and envious because they also want to have the gifts and the anointing God has blessed you with. These people have mastered the art of deceit. Beware!

5. *Spiritual vampires* add no value to your life. In fact, they suck the very life out of you. They are sometimes referred to as Debbie downers. As they enter your air space, they always bring a cloud of despair. They have this woe-is-me syndrome. They suck the joy out of a great day with their negative presence. They have no joy at all. They whine and complain about everything. Nothing is good, and they want you to live in their world of self-pity. They consume massive amounts of your time. Everybody is against them, and your counsel will never satisfy them. They will be back for more. They are miserable and love company. You will actually feel sorry for them. Love and pray for these folks from a distance!
6. *Enemy-in-me* is the most dangerous of all the previously discussed friends. This is a very common foe. Literally, it is the enemy that lurks in the shadows of our own hearts. Most people have a self-destruct mode. It is like you cannot see yourself doing anything positive or different or being successful. The rationale for this kind of thinking can be filtered through a myriad of reasons, including negative preadolescent programming, poor parental scaffolding, or toxic home environments in some cases. Other reasons may include low self-esteem (how you feel about yourself), poor self-image (how you see yourself),

> or fear of success or fear of failure, which are actually one in the same. There is no success without failure. Failure is the pasture for the flowers of success. I have coined this expression: "failure is the framework for the art of success!"

Before, I discuss this next session, I want to be crystal clear. Pressing into the power of God precludes that you are in a place of trying to fulfill God's will for your life. In short, pressing into the power of God is yielding or surrendering your will for the will of the Father. It is always a life-altering experience. Case in point, God wants to take you someplace you have never been and have not conceived in your heart. This will not be an easy transition by any stretch of the imagination. It will test your resolve to serve the Lord. These are the journeys you will take with God that will be indelibly ingrained in your heart.

Thus, in order to accomplish your purpose and obtain divine success in life, you have to confront and destroy three deadly and menacing internal foes: doubt, defeatism, and trepidation. Doubt works against our faith and the finished work of Jesus Christ. Defeatism is an attitude that causes one to give up before they get started. It exalts the plans of the enemy and every potential obstacle or hindrance in an attempt to prevent you from walking by faith to complete a God-given task. Moses had an acute case of this spirit, as seen when

God asked him to deliver the children of Israel from the bondages of Egypt. Trepidation is the anticipation of the fear of doing something. If left unchecked, it will make you tentative, apprehensive, faithless, and always second-guessing the will of God for your life.

They work together as a trio of internal havoc and chaos. Together, they are a more than formidable nemesis. They are tethered to our past through an extensive network of people who were assigned to us at various intervals and pockets of our lives by the enemy. They were assigned to subtly plant the one seed necessary for self-destruction. After being fooled at Calvary once, the enemy takes no chances. He relentlessly puts people in your life to systematically deprogram the hard drive of your mind or your prefrontal cortex to deceive you at pivotal times in your life. The prefrontal cortex essentially helps us to make the proper executive decisions concerning life. I can literally recall at least three teachers—one in elementary school in the third grade at an impressionable stage, one in my freshman year of high school, and one in my senior year of college, during a critical time in my life—who said I would never amount to anything.

If you reflect long enough, you will recall both actions of rejection and words of rejection that you heard and internalized. It is common to think you have dismissed these events, but they have lingered like despair in the basement of your heart, privately lurking in the recesses of your mind, coming together to form a league of personal impediments called doubt, defeatism, and trepidation. They are stealthy, mysteriously drifting in and out of the darkness of our souls—only long enough to release a virus into our spirits that derails us silently and undetected. Then they disappear until the next time we face the hurdle of a major obstacle or the closure of a divine test—a test we have been failing for years. This trio cannot be unveiled naturally. They can only be exposed or revealed spiritually by God Himself. They are spiritual weights, chains of bondage that must be put aside before you can succeed in fulfilling your purpose.

This trio must be confronted by the power of the blood of the Lamb and the words of your testimony. We have carried these psychological and emotional chains of bondage in our spirits for way too long. And every time you get strong enough to break them, someone will say or do something to reinforce their grip over your life. All words have power, and every negative action has a corresponding consequence. Thus, we cannot ignore the injuries left in their wake. We must allow the balm of Gilead to heal us. Next, we must learn to combat and defeat them in spiritual warfare before they jump to the next generation.

Let me help you. It has been said that sticks and stones will break my bones, but words will never hurt me. This is a lie from the pit of hell. In fact, this proverbial antidote was given to my generation and taught to deflect negative words being spoken over our lives by peers and adults alike. The intentions of this antidote were good, but it is not theologically grounded in God. However, this is a good example of a principle one of my former pastors and mentors, the late Bishop Lewis T. Tait Sr., shared with me decades ago to help me understand the nature of truth. A half of a truth is a whole lie. My spiritual father would say that this "sticks and stones" statement falls under the determinate of the law of first truth. Basically, the first thing you were told about a particular subject matter becomes your truth even if it is a verifiable lie. OK, here is the simple truth and real intent of that poem. I did some research on this often misread, misinterpreted, misquoted poem that can be traced back to around 1862. Here is the actual poem by Ruby Redfort, written with its original context:

> Sticks and stones may break my
> bones, but words can also hurt me.
> Stones and sticks break only skin, while
> words are ghosts that haunt me.
> Slant and curved the word-swords
> fall, it pierces and sticks inside me.
> Bats and bricks may ache through
> bones, but words can mortify me.
> Pain from words has left its' scar,
> on mind and hear that's tender.

Cuts and bruises have not healed,
it's words that I remember.

This poem seemly has its roots and principles grounded in Proverbs 18:21 (KJV), "Death and life are in the power of the tongue: and they that love it shall eat the fruit thereof." Our words have power, and we have to choose them wisely. As you battle the enemy within, take the time to search your heart, mind, and soul for words that linger from your past and are tethered to your future. As you press into the power, ask God to free you from the bondage of fermenting negative words spoken over you in your past. Be set free by the power of God to break every yoke of bondage. Walk in the newly discovered freedom of God. Embrace and enjoy a future unencumbered by the words that once hindered your growth and development.

We have to be clear in our understanding. When God made us, He gave all of us our own individual and exclusive assignments. God considered all of the elements that would hinder or preclude us aborting our assignments. He has factored in our sins, shortcomings, and thorns in the flesh. He has even factored in things like abuse, suicidal tendencies, intelligence, betrayals, growing up in the hood, or growing up with a silver spoon. God left no stones unturned and no possible variables or outcomes unaddressed. His sovereignty cannot be destabilized by the seeming uncertainties of life. Nothing is nebulous, vague, or uncertain to our God! Therefore, we must learn to trust God and to lean not to our own understandings. In all our ways, we must acknowledge Him and allow Him to direct our paths (Proverbs 3:6 NKJV). God does not give us assignments we cannot fulfill. We have to learn ways to become an advocate for ourselves, lifting up the inherent victory that lives in us through Christ Jesus our Lord. "Lord, help us! Build a hedge around the enemy in me such that it cannot harm or hinder the Spirit of God in me at work on your behalf, in Jesus's name. Amen!"

CHAPTER 12

SELF-ADVOCACY

BECOME AN ADVOCATE FOR YOURSELF WITH CLARITY OF ASSIGNMENT

There is a common mistake that people in the church make concerning being humble. We all should want to be humble, and we should demonstrate humility as a part of our Christian witness. In fact, I believe in this so much that I coined this phrase that I have lived by for years: "humility is the platform for exaltation." Clearly, in order to go up in life, we must first go down. Herein lies the problem. Sometimes we get too comfortable with being down. When Moses was in exile in Midian, God spoke to him to be Israel's deliverer. He responded in such a way that negated the power of God. He completely attempted to avoid the call of God. His first argument was in relationship to his credibility as an ambassador. Then his second argument referred to his speech impediment, and finally, his third argument revolved around God finding another candidate for the job. We can see a form of humility in play. However, we also need to understand when God is calling us to the front lines. When you hear His voice, you cannot denounce, deflect, or abdicate the responsibility of the call of God on your life. The paralytic and his team rose to the challenge.

We must rise to the occasion, knowing that if God chose us, we can fulfill the assignment. Using the excuse that I am a behind the scenes type of person may really be a smokescreen for rebellion or fear. Neither are acceptable in the grand scheme of God's plan. Case in point, we are capable of turning the divinity of humility into the demonic place that is likened unto Lo-debar. Lo-debar is a place of death, desolation, and dejection. It literally means no pasture, no word, no communication. Lo-debar is "no everything." It is a lifeless and barren place. It was a place of self-loathing captivity for the grandson of King Saul, Mephibosheth. Mephibosheth was also the son of David's best friend, Jonathan. In spite of his lineage being a direct descendent of royalty, Mephibosheth found himself in the most despicable place mentally, spiritually, and emotionally. He was royalty, but he was broke, busted, disgusted, and lame in his feet. Like Moses, the self-exiled fugitive murderer, broken, he could no longer see his value to God. When King David came to restore him to his rightful position, Mephibosheth literally referred to himself as a dead dog.

He was royalty, but he couldn't move. He lived beneath His privilege because he thought he had been forgotten and forsaken. When you land in this space, you have a very difficult time seeing any good in yourself. Your eyes are visually impaired by despair and what seemingly feels like neglect. There are people that see how blessed and anointed you are; however, you have sunk to a such a low place in your spirit where you fail to see what they see. You have been blinded by the darkness of your spiritual position. Years ago, this was a place of humility, but now it has become a debilitating fortress of hopelessness. It seems like your season has come and gone. You feel as if you are permanently ostracized and isolated from the possibility of change. The keys to your future have seemingly been misplaced in time, and God has forgotten about you. Take courage! God will never forget about you! He still has a plan for your life!

Like King David, "I declare that you have to rise out of these ashes!" God has found you. Remember this: in God's eyes, you were never lost. He knows that you felt like Mephibosheth. He knows someone dropped you on your head and injured you. Someone you loved mistreated you and abused the relationship, and now you are spiritually lame. However, God knows you are royalty, and He has come to restore you to your rightful position in Him. Your injury and position in life was never meant to be permanent. It is time for you to join God and to become an advocate for yourself, especially since you were created in His image. Go dust yourself off! It's time to arrive at your destination for purpose. As my spiritual daughter once said, "It's time to shake it off!" Shake off your negative disposition. Shake off the spirit of fear, desperation, and mental anguish. Walk in forgiveness because your appointed time has come!

There are many people in the body of Christ who have been taken captive by the thoughts of others. They are bound by what other people think about them. The roots of these imaginary boundaries are demonic in nature. You cannot allow people to dictate the exact amount of your self-worth based on their diminutive or myopic opinion of you. Oftentimes, what people see in you is a distorted view of what God has formed in you. There is greatness inside of each of us, and we have to loose the ropes and bonds of insecurity and start believing in the plans and promises that God established for us from the very foundation of the world.

"Greater is He that is in you than he who is in the world!" (1 John 4:4 NASB). No one can stop what God has determined to do through you. No one can reorder the steps you have been purposed and authorized to follow. It is time for you to speak up and out. At the same time, you must become an advocate for yourself because of the God that lives and has His being inside of you! God has need of you, and you must awaken like a lion from its afternoon siesta! The time is now! Do not wait for perfect conditions, for they will elude you like a summer breeze.

The lies of the enemy will weigh you down and burden you with the need for external approval. However, when you stand from your place of humility and intimacy before God, whatever God said to you in that space is final. His will for your life is now backed by the leverage and equity of heaven and His divine authority. All things will line up, both good and bad, to fulfill His will. What people think about you is irrelevant. What you think negatively about yourself will eventually pass away. If God has to send four people to carry you and help you obtain His objective for your life, then as incredulous as that may sound, so be it.

When your season comes, there are no obstacles formed that will be able to confront the will of God in and on your life. Like the paralytic, your inner self will awaken. Your inadequacies will no longer be insurmountable hurdles. Your request for assistance will be filled. The crowds will part for you like the Red Sea. The clamor of distractors will be silenced. Position and proximity gaps will be closed. Moreover, the roof of impossibility that seemed impenetrable will be breeched by your determination to fulfill the will of God for your life.

This is a vision of your now, a pronouncement of your freedom and your emancipation from the manipulation of humanity and the spirit of witchcraft. Run! You are free. Don't ever let anyone own that much real estate in your head or heart! Now, run to the Father and show yourself. Get your new marching orders from God and don't look back! The dreams and plans of God have been released from heaven over your life. It's your season. It's your time. The devil will try to hold you, but the devil is a liar. Your freedom was purchased a long time ago on the cross. You were purchased with the blood of a perfect lamb!

As Paul once said, "Stand fast therefore in the liberty by which Christ has made us free, and do not be entangled again with a yoke of bondage" (Galatians 5:1 NKJV). At some point, the paralytic man became an advocate for himself and the plans of God for his life. He convinced the men to escort him to Jesus, and the rest is history. Your past and your present condition have to join your future and surrender to the power of Almighty God! Finally, nothing else matters except fulfilling the will of God for your life. Remember, a renewed mind will restore your focus. The thorns of bitterness no longer pierce your heart. What can you render to God for His many benefits to you? Yes, breathe! Inhale and exhale. Rest in the will of the Father. My spiritual father would say it like this, "Every season of captivity has an expiration date." Now, "let your light so shine before men, that they may see your good works and glorify your Father which is in heaven" (Matthew 5:16 KJV).

Now that you know the chains of powerlessness have been destroyed, it is time to examine who you are in Christ. You have an entire arsenal of spiritual weapons at your disposal. You have always had them. It just was not the right season for activation. Now is your time! This is God's vision for your life. Like all of the biblical characters of notoriety, there is a time, a place, and a season for your spiritual gestation. Gestation is the period of birthing. It is a period of going from just a concept in the mind of God to being a vessel meek for His purposes. It is a period of obscurity where God hides you on purpose until the reveal. That season is usually a traumatic one. However, traumatic seasons can give birth to new realities and good endings. Ask Mephibosheth. The negative effects of traumatic times in our lives always yield to God's intended purpose.

God is sovereign, and His plans are not altered by traumatic events. In fact, trauma enhances divine outcomes. I have created a phrase to describe the period from spiritual gestation to birth. God gave me this concept of a "traumatic triumph." It is the period in your life that is filled with trauma, and yet it produces the stages of growth necessary for your spiritual maturation. *Oxford* defines trauma as "a deeply distressing or disturbing experience." This experience is usually life altering and gut-wrenching. It is an indescribable pain that hurts at the core of your bowels. It will cause you to cry out to God without the solace of tears. It can cause you to scream from the depths of your heart without any accompanying sound except the indescribable sound of anguish. However, remember, there can be no gestation process without pain and discomfort. It is part of your process. Again, as stated earlier, it produces the stages of growth necessary for your spiritual maturation. No fruit is good to eat until it has matured or ripened. At that point, it is ready for the harvest. You thought you were already ready and already ripe for the harvest. Those were simply your thoughts and not God's thoughts. Hold on to this biblical paradigm: "His ways are not like our ways; but, as far as the heavens are from the earth" (Isaiah 55:9 NKJV).

So, if you have been perturbed with God, let it go! God knows exactly what He is doing. He has preserved you during your traumatic experience. You didn't die in your winter season because you were kept by the grace of God for a season and a time such as this! Your trauma has given you your promotion. Begin to praise God! You have survived some of the most horrific chapters of your life. However, your horrors are going to bless the body of Christ. Jesus has shared some of the same afflictions that you are currently experiencing or have already endured. Our experiences must mirror His experiences in order to truly be a part of His body. If Christ, being the head, suffers trauma, then the body of Christ must suffer trauma as well. More importantly, when Christ gets the victory, His body will get the victory as well! The stress and infliction of mental, emotional, and sometimes physical pain and suffering releases the power of God in your life.

The paralytic had to have a prolonged season of lying on his bed. I am sure that in his humanity, he wondered if he would ever walk again—dreaming about a different future with mobility; going through the roller coaster of gaining hope and losing hope; saying yes to the will of God and at the same time feeling sorry for himself. This self-loathing literally zapped the emotional and physical strength he needed to fulfill the will of God over His life, but he pressed through. He is no different from the woman with the issue of blood or the man at the pool of Bethesda. You must come to the revelation that this new birth can only come from and through the divine birth canal of God. Humankind cannot deliver you this time! The destiny of the paralytic was perfected and sealed before the four men ever showed up in his life! If not those four men, then some other group or some other way, but he was destined to walk again—just like you shall live and not die. Today you will declare the works of your God, pandemic or no pandemic. Today the heavens celebrate your release and your new birth.

This leads us into a discussion about the power of you. Of course, God is sovereign, and there is absolutely no one thing in existence, seen or unseen, that compares to Him. He is the one and only Supreme God—and guess what? He created us all! He made us in His image and blessed us to have dominion (Genesis 1:26 NKJV)! We need to walk in the fulness of that image and give Him the glory He deserves by fulfilling the call and purposes of God in our lives. We are "fearfully and wondrously made." There has to be something very special about us.

He created everything else and spoke it into existence, but He made us and breathed into our nostrils the breath of life (Genesis 2:7 NKJV). Our creation was very intentional, hands-on, and calculated. He even stores the treasure of His Spirit in us that He might get the glory if we submit to His will. Let's examine 2 Corinthians 4:7 NKJV, "But we have this treasure in earthen vessels, that the excellence of the power may be of God and not of us." There is power in us. God puts this power in us so He can get the glory. Thus, it makes it a priority for us to learn how to utilize this power. Hence, we need to press into the power and bring God the glory!

In the story of the paralytic and his crew, there is a need to find another access point into the building. The transport team and the paralytic need to go higher in order to reach Jesus. In the same way, we need to go higher in our relationship with God. Our normal access points are no longer viable or sustainable. In other words, we need to learn how to press through spiritual droughts. There are times in our lives when everything seems to have dried up. Spiritual winters are when everything around us is dead and cold. These analogies represent a very lonely season. However, we were designed to survive both spiritual droughts and winters. Whether we are walking through the valley of the shadow of death; in a fiery furnace; the lion's den; being persecuted for no reason; in prison; dealing with church hurt; being abased; on the backside of a desert or in the belly of a whale, we will always be survivors in Christ Jesus our Lord. Our worship and prayer life has to be developed. Worship and prayer grow best in painful and traumatic situations. Likewise, our anointing only grows through the viscosity of the trials and tribulations of life.

The paralytic could have said, "Hey, this is a waste of time. Take me home!" Instead, they endured this impossible situation until someone came up with an ingenious idea that they executed to perfection and found themselves in the presence of the greatest teacher, preacher, priest, and prophet to ever walk the face of the earth, Jesus. Pressing to get into His presence and power was more than worth the price of admission. Remember this: we need to go higher because our ordinary access points into the presence of God will be blocked. We always say, "God is doing a new thing!" In the meanwhile, we attempt to do the same old thing. Listen, if God is doing a new thing, then the body must follow the lead of the head of the church. Do some things differently so you can catch up to God!

The roof in the story represents the limitations of life, and some of them are self-imposed. In many instances, we look at the challenges and obstacles of life and count ourselves out before we get started. That's why we don't accomplish anything. We talk ourselves out of the blessing and the promise. Many of us are just like the paralyzed man at the pool of Bethesda. We are waiting for all the circumstances and conditions to be perfect in order to get into the pool. Here is a prime example of God changing directions, in the sense that He decided to come help this man personally instead of using an angel. Normal access points were cut off. God stepped into his condition and his imperfection to do a perfect work.

We have failed to learn the most basic lessons of Genesis 1:1–2, and that is that God does His best work in darkness and chaos. The paralytic and his team just figured out that where there is a will, there is a way. God will make a way out of no way, and we must possess that same attribute. People often say, "Think outside of the box," and that is good. However, kingdom thinking says to elevate your thinking. So I say, "Think as if there is no box!" The paralytic and his team were rewarded for their efforts! How many people do you know who have witnessed a miracle or been in earshot of Jesus's power and presence?

In your lowest moments in this season, you will encounter the presence of God and obtain His power. Just remember that while you are in pursuit of God, you may experience some of the lowest moments of your life, but don't quit. This is only a test! Keep praying! Keep reading! Keep loving God and His people. Keep the faith! Don't stop moving! Don't stop believing! Time is not your enemy. Time is the workshop of God's plans.

It will always be used to the glory of God! When we are aligned with the will of God, time will become an ally.

The devil always tries to burden you with the idea that time is your enemy. It is not too late. Your door of opportunity has not closed. Time is our friend. Time works for God. The plans of God take time into consideration and compel time to work on our behalf. We are forgiven, and it is time to pick up our problems and walk with them into our destiny. We have the power of God now. God has some surprises in store for us in the very near future if we "walk by faith and not by sight" (2 Corinthians 5:17 NKJV).

One of these things is learning how to cultivate new relationships without burning the bridges of former relationships. A new, improved, and more mature version of you should realize that as God does a new thing in your life, it may require a different network of people. This does not mean that the relationships you had get tossed away like an old shoe. No. All relationships, good and bad, need to be cherished as the "necessary will of God." Judas was necessary in the life of Jesus. In order to fulfill scripture, Jesus needed a betrayer with a deadly kiss, and Judas was that man. Without that kiss, things might not have turned out in our favor. Who would have died for our sins? Don't underestimate the power of that kiss. The kiss identified Jesus and destined Him for the crucifixion and the resurrection. Without the shedding of blood, there would be no forgiveness of sins. Don't underestimate the sovereign will of God to manipulate negativity to bring about positive results.

More than a half century of living has afforded me the opportunity to accrue much wisdom. I have come to understand that we are the compendium of all the people who have interacted in our lives, both negatively and positively. Everyone played a role. Thus, everyone was an absolute necessity. My mother was a domestic when she moved north from the South. She worked for a very prominent Jewish family. She told me that every morning, they used an uplifting superlative to encourage their children. When these children grew up, they all walked in the manifestation of those words. She adopted that same philosophical and biblical approach with my sister and me. I believed we both turned out OK.

Ponder these thoughts: people do matter, and as you cultivate new relationships, be selective about who you have in your space. Make sure they have the capacity to carry your mat and the spirit to engage and embrace the promises that God has given you! Do not allow people to occupy space in your life for negative loitering and prying. People in your space should have your best interest at heart. If they do not possess the capacity to help you navigate the bridge over troubled waters, then you are not obligated to share your personal space with them.

THE CONCLUSION: BY INVITATION ONLY

It is critically important that we understand that pressing into the power of God is not some kind of quick fix. It is a time-released period of perfecting alignments, whereby our will lines up with the will of God for our lives. It is not something that can be done with sheer human will. It cannot be forced. If it is forced, it would be the equivalent of putting a square block into a round hole. In other words, you cannot make this season happen. It would be premature and of no effect. No, the act of pressing into the power of God can only be done through the power of the Holy Spirit and the will of God. You cannot make this happen. There are absolutely too many variables that have to be in place that literally have to be divinely orchestrated. When you are called into this place of pressing and spiritual maturity, your life will be processed in ways that were inconceivable or unfathomable to your imagination. If God had asked you to volunteer for this assignment, your answer would have been, "Absolutely not." Thus, God did not make a request. He uses our proclivity to sin or the pathways of life as a conduit for this divine bootcamp from hell.

At times, it seems both unbearable and inescapable, but, like Job, you will survive. Herein lies the irony. People love the story of Job and the latter glory of Job. However, very few people would have endured Job's pain to embrace his testimony.

The pain of process is part of the press. In this stage, your life may take an absolute turn for the worst, like the life of Joseph. Can you imagine the sheer emotional pain and turmoil of what it felt like to be stripped and put in a pit to be sold as an object of human trafficking by your own brothers? When Joseph left his father, do you think he thought for one minute that it would be the last time he would see his father, sleep in his bed, or enjoy the pleasures of freedom in a familiar cultural context? It would be over a decade and some years before Joseph would be able to engage his family. Even with the inherent problems in his dysfunctional family, I am sure that this kind of rejection and duplicity never crossed his mind. When Joseph left that morning, it was just another day in the life of a shepherding family. He was merely following his father's mandate and conforming to his usual behavior of snitching on his brothers.

Instead, it was the day of his processing. It was going to be the first day of the press. He would meet betrayal, jealousy, and envy face-to-face. He would confront his worst fears. Tears and anger would combine for a toxic cocktail of mixed emotions and uncertainty. On this day, he would begin a thirteen-year journey to the place where his gifts would make room for him and bring him before great men. He did not ask to be kidnapped with intent to become the prince of Egypt, because he could have never imagined this elevation. Even his dreams could not describe the personal angst of this manifestation, simply because this was not his will. It was the will of God. It was mandated in heaven from the foundation of the world.

These plans could not be intercepted by men. These plans could not be created by men. They were instead the plans that represent the ingenious "bara force" of God. The bara force is the creative will of God. The Hebrew origin of the word *bara* is to create, so I coined the phrase "*bara force*" when I was pastoring to describe the creative will of God. Thus, the creative plan of pressing into the power of God was wielded in the inception and conception of the mind of God. In context, inception is the genesis of something, the point of origin, or the evolution of an idea that is only conceivable in the mind of God, the Progenitor, or our Antecedent God. Meanwhile, conception is putting a plan in motion to make the inception or the idea a reality.

Hence, this process concerning the birth and development of a divine plan that involves you is by invitation only. God will order your steps to bring you down the right path at the right time. He will surround you with the right friends. He will remove people from your life. The calling to press into His power is by design and by invitation only. When I was an undergraduate student at Howard University, I learned a term to describe this event, called *zeitgeist*. In a theological context, it is the interface of the Spirit of God and a specific moment in time to create context for the will of God. It is an appointed time or the fulness of time. It is the perfect storm. You could not design a plot this intricate if you had a thousand years of preparation. God will allow you to have the featured role in His production if you are willing to say yes after you have sunken to epic lows in your life. It is hard to look up from the most difficult and compromising situations of your life and say yes, but if you manage to hear his voice and to respond in the affirmative, a life-transforming process will commence!

Joseph was a type of Christ. He ultimately surrendered his will while in prison, as evidenced by his treatment of his brothers after his incarceration. He understood that this catastrophic event worked together for the salvation of Israel during what would have been considered an international crisis event. Israel would have perished had Joseph not been in a position of authority. However, note that Joseph had to lose his life to gain it. Unfortunately, we do not have a greater context of understanding for the paralytic man. However, I'm sure that coming home healed after all those years changed his family and his network and his surrounding community. His miracle brought someone hope. We do not know the depth of intricacy woven into the life of this paralytic.

We do know it was profound enough to be featured in this book and the Bible. This story will be read by billions of sojourners who need to know that God will do something special for those who press into His power. Watching the power and the equity or assets of heaven open up over the paralytic's life will bless countless lives of people who will endure the struggle to press.

As I close, Christ then becomes the ultimate icon for pressing into the power of God. He was militant and radical in His approach to the faith. He was definitively not in the business of making the powers that be happy. He so agitated the members of the status quo in His community that the first time He preached, they wanted to push Him off of a cliff. For three years, He was a thorn in the side of the social and spiritual elite. He became such a public nuisance that they conspired to kill Him. It was on the night of His arrest that He experienced some of the lowest seasons or epochs of His life. During the Last Supper with his disciples, Judas sealed his own fate. He determined that he was going to hand Jesus over to his conspirators. All Jesus ever did was love, teach, and bless these men with the gift of God through divine obedience. As noted earlier, the ensuing kiss of death was a blessing in disguise.

Before this event transpired, Jesus was praying with great distress in the garden. His disciples were supposed to be praying with Him, but they fell asleep. Thus, He was essentially alone. It was just Jesus and His Father.

When you are pressing into the presence of God, it will be just you and the Father. God does not have an assignment for your team. The assignment requires you to walk the rest of the process out alone. This was only the beginning of the crucible for Jesus—a crucial, life-altering moment where help only comes from the Lord. During this process, no one will truly understand the metamorphosis you are experiencing. The fire of your trials is altering you forever in preparation for your next dimension of ministry. This phenomenon cannot be explained. In order to grow spiritually, we will have to endure these experiences. This crucible is divine and customized just for you. These customized situations cannot be escaped through human ingenuity but only endured through the manifest will of God. Jesus is experiencing one of these moments in the Garden of Gethsemane.

The Aramaic derivative of the word Gethsemane means *oil press*. It was the place of His pressing. It was here that He prayed until He sweated drops of blood. On the converse, His most trusted disciples could not keep their eyes open. I guess they suffered from postprandial somnolence or what is commonly called itis. Nevertheless, they were not present to understand the depth of pressure Jesus was under in this press. Even if they were right by His side, they would not have been subject to an understanding of Jesus's process. Watching someone else's process is not the same as going through your own process. No one was to experience this pressurized extraction of the oil of His anointing but Jesus. He was destined to become our sacrificial Lamb, taking on all the sins of humanity, only to become our resurrected, triumphant High Priest. It was by design and customized just for Jesus. In short, no one could endure this kind of agonizing torment for the sins of the world but Jesus.

The scripture captures this moment of pressing with riveting details in Luke 22:39–48 (NLT):

> Then, accompanied by the disciples, Jesus left the upstairs room and went as usual to the Mount of Olives. There he told them, "Pray that you will not give in to temptation." He walked away, about a stone's throw, and knelt down and prayed, "Father, if you are willing, please take this cup of suffering away from me. Yet I want your will to be done, not mine." Then an angel from heaven appeared and strengthened him. He prayed more fervently, and he was in such agony of spirit that his sweat fell to the ground like great drops of blood. At last he stood up again and returned to the disciples, only to find them asleep, exhausted from grief. "Why are you sleeping?" he asked them.

> "Get up and pray, so that you will not give in to temptation." But even as Jesus said this, a crowd approached, led by Judas, one of his twelve disciples. Judas walked over to Jesus to greet him with a kiss. But Jesus said, "Judas, would you betray the Son of Man with a kiss?"

This kiss would signify a mark of authority and distinction, an assignment of deity in the earth, sonship, divine obedience, kingship, elevation, and press that actually caused Jesus to demonstrate His manifest purpose in the earth. These designations were not necessary for God but for the world to know and to acknowledge the love of God that was so deep He sent His Son to die on the cross for our sins. His Son, Jesus, would then be buried in a borrowed tomb after He demonstrated what it meant to press into the power of God, submitting His will and exchanging it for the will of God. When we press into the power, we have to surrender our will. Trust God, and whatever His plans are, we will be fine with the divine outcomes. Pressing into His power is acknowledging that you cannot help yourself. It is an acceptance of the governance of God. Listen to this declaration" "God, I don't know where we are going, but I trust your ways and your leadership." This transference of personal governance to divine governance can occur multiple times in your life on both small and large scales.

I have personally had this encounter with God on at least four occasions. My first time was in April 1984, when I surrendered my life to Christ after realizing that I was on a collision course with self-destruction. My second time pressing into the power of God revolved around my call to ministry in the summer of 1986. Two years later, I would be releasing my lifelong dream of being an attorney and accepting the invitation to enroll in divinity school. This was a pivotal point in my life because I had already been accepted into two law schools. I had worked my entire life for that opportunity. There were two men at that time who helped to carry my mat: my mentor and longtime friend Dr. Lewis T. Tait Jr. and Dr. Cain Hope Felder, who eventually became a lifelong mentor as well. They walked me to the roof of decision, and I decided to follow God. My life has never been the same.

My third transition came in October 1999, when I was prompted by God, during a twenty-one-day absolute fast, to resign from my first pastoral assignment from a prominent denominational church and to start a nondenominational church in the basement of my home, New Vision International Ministries. With the succor of my spiritual father, Bishop Vaughn Mclaughlin, the support of my scaffolding and praying wife and family, and the dedication of many teams of selfless individuals, the church has grown from that initial meeting of fourteen people in a 300-square-foot space to a robust ministry of more than eight hundred people that is now housed in a two-story 65,000-square-foot building. It is a miraculous story of the extraordinary power of God. Pressing into the power is never easy, and I don't want to lead you down a path of false bliss. Pressing into the power will and can cause mental anguish, bouts with your greatest fears and uncertainty, confrontation of personal sins and repentance, painful personal and public transformation, and finally divine redemption. That was just a simple overview of the process, because the granular details need to be preserved for another book.

My fourth encounter was an unprecedented move that made the purchase of that new facility possible and set the table for apostolic succession. Once again, I was called to press into the power of God as I was tasked with relinquishing my responsibilities as senior pastor and turning the helm of the church over to my spiritual son and daughter. Lead Pastor Dexter and Lady Lindsey Upshaw are currently doing an amazing job leading the transition to the aforementioned facility from our first purchase of a 15,600-square-foot building on an 85,000-square-foot campus. It was in my obedience to leave the work God started that God began to move in ways that were a continuation of the vision He gave me back in 1997. My wife and I then pursued the call of God, coming to Jacksonville, Florida, to work at the Potter's House International Ministries under the pastoral leadership of my spiritual parents, Bishop Vaughn and Lady Narlene McLaughlin.

Finally, I am again pressing into the power of God again as I write this book, not because I have the ability but because of a divine metamorphic process that is leading me from the call of ministry to the pursuit of purpose. My life is being transitioned and transformed every day. God is doing a new thing, and I am making adjustments daily as I attempt to follow His lead. I have no idea what the outcomes are going to be. I just know that I have to follow God to have any outcome at all. This is not an easy transition, because I am over fifty and have had to reset all of my ways. I have discovered that God is not interested in me being comfortable. Following God can be totally uncomfortable and unnerving in the sense of traversing unfamiliar territory. I have never been down this path before. My wife and I have clasped our hands together and closed our eyes. We are taking yet another leap of faith and are committed to this journey. This is not to be taken literally in the sense of a lack of preparation and prayer. On the contrary, it requires more preparation and hours of strategic prayer. The book of James reminds us that faith without works is dead. I am sure my wife has her own story to tell.

However, from my perch, I am literally on the Potter's wheel, seemingly spinning out of control, and yet I have to trust the guiding and seasoned hands of the Potter.

God is the Potter, and He knows exactly what He is doing. I realize with the writing and release of this book that my life will never be the same, but I have to press into His power, and whatever emerges as an outcome will be fine with me and bring glory to God. Millions have read and will read the story of the paralytic man and his crew and glean from their unrelenting pursuit of God. Millions will also continue to glorify God because this man came through the roof of despair and desperation lame. He then encountered the presence of Jesus and walked out of the door of opportunity, rejoicing in the power of Almighty God. This is a testimony to what happens when you press into the power of God! When the opportunity comes, don't ever be afraid to press into the power of God. It will change your life from the mundane to the miraculous. Ask me how I know!

#PressIntoThePower

*ADDENDUM PRAYER

Lord, as I go through the pain of fleshly withdrawal and uncertainty in pursuit of my purpose and Your glory, let this book become a resource to church leaders all over the world. Let it be a yoke-breaking and inspirational read that pushes people to their purposes in the kingdom of God internationally. Moreover, Lord, let it be a source of encouragement for the next generation and a strategic map for the next vanguard. In Jesus's name. Amen!

Made in the USA
Columbia, SC
05 January 2023